Myths and Mysteries of Wayland Smith

Myths and Mysteries *of* Wayland Smith

Clive Alfred Spinage

WYCHWOOD PRESS

Our books may be ordered from bookshops or (post free) from
Jon Carpenter Publishing, Alder House, Market Street, Charlbury, OX7 3PH
Tel/fax 01608 811969

e-mail: wychwood@joncarpenter.co.uk

Credit card orders should be phoned or faxed to 01689 870437 or 01608 811969

Please send for our free catalogue

OXFORDSHIRE LIBRARY SERVICE

3 200430 859	
WYCHWOOD PRESS	23/7/03
	£10.00
⟨	

First published in 2003 by

The Wychwood Press

an imprint of Jon Carpenter Publishing

Alder House, Market Street, Charlbury, Oxfordshire OX7 3PH

© Clive Alfred Spinage. The right of Clive Alfred Spinage to be identified as author of this work has been asserted in accordance with the Copyright, Design and Patents Act 1988

All rights reserved. No part of this publication may be reproduced, stored in a retrieval system or transmitted in any form or by any means electronic, mechanical, photocopying or otherwise without the prior permission in writing of the publisher

ISBN 1 902279 16 6

Printed in England by Antony Rowe Ltd., Eastbourne

Contents

Chapter 1	In the Mists of Time	1
Chapter 2	Wayland's Smithy	41
Chapter 3	Origins of the Wayland Smith Legend	58
Chapter 4	Stories of the Norsemen	70
Chapter 5	Scott's Story	78
Postscript		86
The Antiquary's Bookshelf		88
Index		89

Illustrations

Plates

1	Wayland's Smithy, 1956.	viii
2	Wayland's Smithy, 1956.	viii
3	A photograph about 1900 of Wayland's Smithy, courtesy Vale and Downland Museum, Wantage.	2
4	Postcard circa 1920s of Wayland's Smithy.	2
5	Postcard circa 1920s of Wayland's Smithy.	3
6	After restoration in 1963, 1999.	4
7	After restoration in 1963, 1999.	4
8	After restoration in 1963, 2002.	5
9	After restoration in 1963, 2002.	5
10	The entrance, 2002.	6
11	The main chamber, 2002.	6
12	The western side-chamber, 1999.	7
13	The eastern side chamber, 1999.	8
14	The view north standing on the chamber.	9
15	View south from the approximate location of *baeahhilde byrigels*. Wayland's Smithy is behind the central clump of trees on the horizon.	14
16	The sarsen stones in front of Ashdown House.	18
17	Ashdown House.	19
18	The stone at Snivelling Corner, 1999.	34
19	The stone at Snivelling Corner, 1999.	34
20	The witch's moon dial with, inset, a sketch of the markings. The base is added for display.	37
21	View from the air, 2000. © English Heritage, National Monuments Record.	42
22	View from the air, 1976, showing the circular crop marks of iron-age dwellings, the ancient line of the Ridgeway, and the track to the north-west. © Crown copyright, National Monuments Record.	43

Figures

1. Contour map of the site showing the north drop of the Downs and Snivelling Corner. 10
2. Illustration of the carving on the Frank's casket. 16
3. The sketch by John Aubrey, 1670. © The Bodleian Library. 20
4. The illustration by Francis Wise, 1738. 20
5. Plan of the site by Lewis 1868, and the supposed arrangement of the sarsen stones at Ashdown. 21
6. Illustration in Lyson's *Magna Britannia*, 1806. 25
7. Illustration from *The Mirror of Literature, Amusement, and Instruction*, July 1826, 'Wayland Smith's Cave', showing fir trees surrounding it. 26
8. Illustration from *The Mirror of Literature, Amusement, and Instruction*, February 1833. 26
9. Illustration of 'Wayland Smith's Cave', probably about 1830. 27
10. Akerman's illustration, 1847. 28
11. Akerman's illustration, 1847. 29
12. Donaldson's illustrations, 1848. 30
13. Illustration in Chamber's *Book of Days*, 1888. 31
14. Artist's impression of the second barrow under construction. The first barrow is shown covered over with the tree trunks left in place. In the second the capstones are not in place. 44
15. Artist's impression of the mummification platform. 46
16. The layout of the barrow after Whittle et al. 1991. 48
17. The 'currency bars' as drawn by Smith in 1920. On the right, their probable mode of use as reinforcement to the point of a stake. 56
18. Cruikshank's impression of Flibbertigibbet. 79
19. Artist's impression in *Kenilworth*, circa 1890. The 'smithy'. 81
20. Artist's impression in *Kenilworth*, circa 1890. Wayland threatens Flibbertigibbet and Tressilian. 81
21. Artist's impression in *Kenilworth*, circa 1890. Wayland in his cave with Flibbertigibbet and Tressilian. 83

Top: Plate 1. Wayland's Smithy, 1956.
Bottom: Plate 2. Wayland's Smithy, 1956.

I
In the Mists of Time

'The schoolmaster is the great enemy of legendary lore.'

Wright, 1847.

An ancient legend

'If you have time to walk down to that little clump of trees over there, towards Aethelred's camp. You will find an old Druidical cromlech well worth examining. It is called Wayland Smith's cave. Walter Scott, who should have known better, says that the Danish king killed at Ashdown was buried there. He was no more buried there than in Westminster Abbey,' wrote Thomas Hughes in 1859 in his book *The Scouring of the White Horse*.

Travel west fourteen furlongs (1½ miles) from that strange landmark of the Berkshire Downs, the Uffington White Horse, along the ancient windswept Ridgeway, and you will see on your right a circle of old beech trees, their branches bending and protesting in the wind. Before its restoration in 1963 'to its appearance in antiquity as far as surviving features allow [except for a flight of stone steps leading onto the top of it]' and now marked by a large Ministry of Public Works explanatory notice board and surrounded by a barbed wire fence, hidden in the gloomy recess of an oval plantation of beech trees and its appearance altered little in the past three hundred years, you would have found a mysterious cavern-like structure of old grey wethers, or sarsen stones. Since time immemorial it has gone by the name of Wayland's Smithy, after the mythical Weland the Smith of Teutonic folklore. Its association with Wayland Smith has made it the most famous of all long barrows in Britain. Writing in 1861 one antiquary stated that for the last two centuries it had been known simply as Wayland Smith, not

Plate 3. A photograph about 1900 of Wayland's Smithy, courtesy Vale and Downland Museum, Wantage.

Plate 4. Postcard circa 1920s of Wayland's Smithy.

In the Mists of Time 3

Plate 5. Postcard circa 1920s of Wayland's Smithy.

Wayland Smith's Cave as the then generation called it. The story among local people of the invisible smith called Wayland, who shod a horse if it was left there with payment placed on the large stone, was known at least in the sixteenth century (Plates 1 to 13).

> The remains, still known locally by these names [Wayland's Smithy or Wayland Smith's Cave], are situated in a wild and lonely place away from any dwelling and within a few yards of the remarkable ancient road known as the Ridgeway, a broad, grassy road which leads up over the hill to Uffington Castle, and forms indeed an important feature in the primitive road-system of Berkshire. Wayland's Cave is situated under a group of lofty beeches which throw a gloomy and romantic shade over a spot of great archaeological interest. The continual breeze passing through the trees produces a low mournful murmur which greatly adds to the impressiveness and solemnity of the place. Upon entering the group of shady trees, one descends into a slight trench or fosse. The actual stones of which the 'cave' is composed are in a somewhat confused condition, but it is still possible to make out the arrangement...

Plates 6 and 7. After restoration in 1963, 1999.

IN THE MISTS OF TIME 5

Plates 8 and 9. After restoration in 1963, 2002.

Top: Plate 10. The entrance, 2003
Bottom: Plate 11. The main chamber, 2002.

Plate 12. The western side chamber, 1999.

Thus wrote George Clinch in 1906 in the *Victoria County History of Berkshire*, giving us a flavour of what it was like at that time.

At more than 700 feet (217 metres) above sea level this Neolithic chambered long barrow, for such it is, is sited at the highest point in the parish of Ashbury just above the northern brow of the Downs (Plate 14), which fall away sharply to the north and west almost 300 feet to Odstone Farm and Ashbury at 417 feet (127 metres) below (Fig. 1). This in itself is uncommon, for most barrows were built in the lowlands. When it was constructed the entrance was by the side of the Ridgeway, but a ditch dug in front of it in Romano-British times resulted in the ancient road being diverted a little away from it.

A legend from the mists of time – possibly originating as early as 1500 B.C. in Mycenean times, becoming Greek, Scandinavian, then early Germanic and Anglo-Saxon, well known in Scandinavia and on the Continent – remarkably the legend of Wayland was only preserved in Britain in Berkshire in the legend of Wayland's Smithy.

Plate 13. The eastern side chamber, 1999.

It was probably brought by the conquering Anglo-Saxons who first arrived in the area in the 5th century. Even then the cromlech might not have been connected with the legend but for the great carved figure in chalk of the mystical White Horse to the east, carved into the Downs 1,000 years after the burial site of Wayland's Smithy ceased to be used. When the first Anglo-Saxons climbed the Berkshire Downs and gazed in wonder upon the White Horse and its nearby cromlech, they must have thought they had found the true site of the legend. The White Horse was surely Sleipnir, the great eight-legged horse of Odin; or perhaps Skemming, Wayland's

Plate 14. The view north, standing on the chamber.

horse, swifter than a bird in flight and 'best of all horses'. Either way, it was testimony to the fact that the place was mystical and important. The cave *must* have been that of Wayland. But he would not have been seen as providing horse-shoes for peasants, but swords and treasures for warriors.

On the other hand, in many parts of the world shy and primitive peoples often do business on the borders of their territories by leaving goods or currency there, returning later to collect other objects in exchange and never showing themselves to the strangers. It has been suggested that such a custom may perhaps have grown up between Romano-Britains and the invading Anglo-Saxons, and this might explain the legend of leaving money on the stone in return for a service, the Anglo-Saxons then giving it the name of Wayland's Smithy for that reason. Another suggestion, made by Michael Bayley, is that the Anglo-Saxons misunderstood the name by which the local Romano-Britains called it, *Wag llan dir ys merthyr*, which in Cornish (i.e. Celtic) dialect translates as 'The

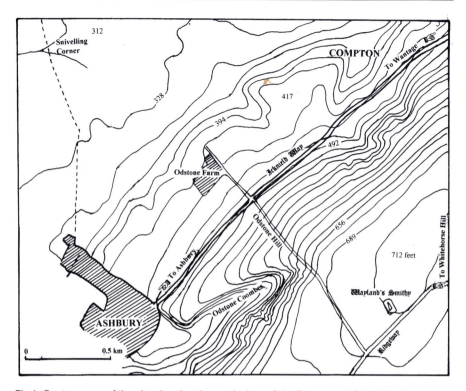

Fig 1. Contour map of the site showing the north drop of the Downs and Snivelling Corner.

burial place beneath the mound of the sacred enclosure of the track', which topographically makes good sense.

The White Horse itself is an artefact which would have demanded regular cleaning to prevent its rapid disappearance under the turf, and thus undoubtedly was maintained even under Roman rule by the Iron Age peoples who constructed it. They probably could not tell the Anglo-Saxon strangers why they maintained it, but the strangers' interest would have encouraged friendly relations and they probably continued under Anglo-Saxon encouragement a maintenance which has existed to the present day.

In the next almost thousand years after the Anglo-Saxons brought the legend to this spot, the cromlech was little known except to curious antiquaries and to the Berkshire shepherds and local people who roamed this part of the Downs, until Sir Walter Scott, one of the great storytellers of the Victorian age, popularised it in his tale *Kenilworth* published in 1821, bringing it to a wide audience despite his corruption of the legend. Scott himself declared he obtained his information from Camden's *Britannia*, and not from his friends the Hughes at Uffington (a little village nestling under the White Horse) as is generally reported, although Mrs. Hughes was described as having a knowledge of the curiosities of county history which was unequalled.

The Hughes had the highest connections. The Reverend Thomas Hughes held royal office and married Mary Anne Watts, daughter and heiress of the Reverend George Watts, vicar of Uffington and son of the Reverend George Watts, chaplain to George II. Their son, John Hughes, later of Donnington Priory, was the father of Tom Hughes, author of *Tom Brown's Schooldays* and *The Scouring of the White Horse*. Tom Hughes's grandmother, known as Madame Hughes, an accomplished musician and singer, was a friend of the Reverend Richard Barham, author of *The Ingoldsby Legends*, as well as of Sir Walter Scott. She obtained tales which she related to both Scott and Barham from her domestic servants, the Reverend Barham recording in his diary for 1829 that Mrs. Hughes had been told by her servant about Snivelling Stone:

> Snivelling Stone, about two miles and half from the cromlech known as Wayland Smith's Cave, in Berkshire, is a large stone, which it is said that Wayland, having ordered his attendant dwarf to go on an errand, and observing the boy to go reluctantly, kicked after him. It just caught his heel, and from the tears which ensued, it derived its traditionary appellation.

On October 10th 1828, seven years after *Kenilworth* had been published, Scott wrote to Mrs. Hughes:

> ...I have thoughts (though it is a *great secret*) of making a revised edition with some illustrations...but to this I would like to add some notice of their present state [i.e. places mentioned in Ashmole's *Antiquities of Berkshire*], & of any traditions which may be still current about them, & for this material addition I

must trust to Mr. John Hughes' and your kindness, as also for some thing, no great matter what, about Wayland Smith's stone; there is no hurry about this...

Mrs. Hughes then sent the information for the new edition and on November 15th he replied:

The notes upon Wayland etc. are exactly what I want and make my task an easy one. For once you have told me of

> a wood
> Where a wood should not be.

[Presumably this referred to the trees planted around the site]. I know of few positions which trees do not ornament but to plant out the curiosities whether of nature or antiquity is certainly a great mistake.

On August 24th 1830 he wrote,

I will be delighted to receive the drawing of Wayland Smith's dwelling which, with the anecdotes you have supplied me with, will make me rich in illustrations of Waverley...' [meaning *Kenilworth* in the Waverley series].

The illustration was never used, however, more fanciful interpretations being afforded by subsequent illustrators, and the text was never altered from the original version. Scott simply added an explanatory note in an appendix 'Author's Notes', which was added to the new edition:

The great defeat, given by Alfred to the Danish invaders, is said, by Mr. Gough [an editor of Camden's *Britannia*], to have taken place near Ashdown, in Berkshire [see below]...
    The popular belief still retains memory of this wild legend, which, connected as it is with the site of a Danish sepulchre,

may have arisen from some legend concerning the northern Duergar, who resided in the rocks, and were cunning workers in steel and iron. It was believed that Wayland Smith's fee was sixpence, and that, unlike other workmen, he was offended if more was offered. Of late his offices have again been called to memory; but fiction has in this, as in other cases, taken the liberty to pillage the stores of oral tradition. This monument must be very ancient, for it has been kindly pointed out to me that it is referred to in an ancient Saxon charter, as a landmark. The monument has been of late cleared out, and made considerably more conspicuous.

Known to the Anglo-Saxons

We first read of the 'smithy' much earlier than this in 955 in one of the ancient Anglo-Saxon Charters, because it lay on the boundary of an estate which became the parish of Compton Beauchamp. The limits were described in a gift of land by King Eadred to Ælfheah his kinsman and minister, apparently the son of Ealdorman Ealhhelm and brother of Ealdorman Ælfhere of Mercia, and of Eadric and Ælfwine. Ælfheah was appointed ealdorman of Hampshire about 959 and died about 972. The boundary description of his gift terminated with the words: *andlang furh op hit cymo on pæt wide geat be eastan welandes smidthan*, 'along the driven furrow till it comes to the wide gate to the east of Weland's Smithy.'

This suggests the earth covering had gone by 955, otherwise it would not have been referred to as Wayland's Smithy. The mound was probably uncovered in the Roman period, either with the destruction of traditional Celtic beliefs under the Roman yoke, the people no longer fearing the gods who might have hitherto protected it, or with the advent of Christianity in the 3rd and 4th centuries. But being of the Stone Age there would have been nothing of value to rob, for the people did not use metals and stone weapons were their most valued possessions. By Bronze Age times things had changed and perhaps gold objects might be found, but the stories of great treasure, especially gold, in burial mounds, as in the Anglo-Saxon

Plate 15. View south from the approximate location of *baeahhilde byrigels*. Wayland's Smithy is behind the central clump of trees on the horizon.

romance of *Beowulf*, possibly derived from legends emanating from pillaging of the tombs of Ancient Egyptians. Of course tomb robbers would not know whether mounds were of Neolithic or later age, and by Anglo-Saxon times funereal rites involved the interment of bodies with much more in the way of earthly treasures.

Nearby, almost two kilometres to the north-west near Hardwell Wood, *hwittuces hlaewe* ('Wittich's Hill') has been suggested as commemorating Wittich, the son of Wayland by Bodvild; and in a charter of 856 *baeahhilde byrigels* ('Beaghild's burial-place') almost four kilometres exactly due north of Wayland's Smithy, somewhere near Cowleaze Farm in Woolstone parish (Plate 15), has been interpreted as the burial place of Bodvild, the princess whom Wayland ravished. Others disagree for grammatical reasons that these names are related to the Wayland legend. In the Celtic tongue *baeahhilde byrigels* could be *beagl-hel-da byrig-kel-ys* – meaning 'the fold and shelter of the ford of the place below of the herdsmen driving cattle' – which makes much more sense, for it is somewhere close to a stream and people would not have buried their dead close to streams for the adjacent fields would have flooded in winter. Likewise there is no obvious mound to mark *hwittuces hlaewe* but there is a spring in the approximate locality, and the Celtic rendering *Gwit* (or *With*)-*tus-cether llawr* would mean 'the stream of the people of the clan of the flat valley land', the spring indeed forming a stream which flows down to the flat land below.

It was formerly thought the legend of Wayland the Smith was known in Northumberland for more than two centuries before it was referred to in the Anglo-Saxon charter, presumably brought from Scandinavia by the Vikings; for a carved whalebone box of alleged Northumbrian workmanship dated as no later than about 700, known as the Franks casket from the name of the person who donated pieces he bought in Paris in 1857 to the British Museum, is carved on the lid and sides with illustrations of apparently popular tales of the time. A runic inscription on it states: 'The flood lifted up the fish on to the cliff-bank; the whale became sad, where he swam on the shingle. Whale's bone.' The front panel of this remarkable survival which had been used as a workbox by a French family until they removed the silver fittings holding it together, depicts an event from the story of Wayland in which he is working on the head of the king's son grasped in his tongs, while the prince's headless body lies below the anvil. With his right hand he offers a cup to Bodvild, who is accompanied by a servant, holding the gold ring which her father, King Nidud, had stolen from Wayland. On the right, Egil, Wayland's brother, is catching birds to make the wings with which Wayland will fly away (see below for the legend). Strangely, this is set next to what has been interpreted as the three wise men bringing gifts to the Virgin and Child, although they have a bird walking with them. Strange because we have a pagan tale on the left and a christian one on the right, but perhaps that is what it is meant to indicate, that christian beliefs had replaced pagan ones.

The carving on the lid has been interpreted by some as depicting Wayland's escape on wings and the righthand could illustrate Egil shooting at birds or at Wayland. But this lays too much stress on the Wayland legend, and one of the most recent interpretations is that it depicts an adaptation of an Homeric myth, one of the battles in the Iliad showing the Trojan offensive led by Hector against the Greek fortifications defended by the archer Teucer, while Achilles sits behind him and sulks, refusing to fight. The runes *aegili* have been

Fig.2. Illustration of the carving on the Frank's casket.

suggested to mean 'one who causes affliction', i.e. shoots arrows into people. The left side panel clearly tells the story of Romulus and Remus, while the back panel depicts the conquering of Jerusalem by Titus and the suppression of the Jews. The tale on the right side panel (which is in the Florence Museum) has not been determined, but one suggestion is that it represents scenes from the Siegfrid Saga with Sigurd's horse Grani bowing its head at its master's death.

The most recent analysis, comparing the carvings with 'picture stones' in Sweden and carved crosses in Northumbria and Yorkshire, suggests the casket dates not from 700, but within 50 years of the year 1000, and was possibly carved in York, one of the cultural centres of the world at that time (Fig. 2).

The antiquaries

After the charter there is a long gap in references to the site perhaps connected with it being related to a pagan myth which would have made it blasphemous to refer to in a christian country, before it is briefly mentioned by the antiquary William Camden in 1586 in his *Britannia*, the first comprehensive topographical survey of England. He stated that the defeat of the Danes by Alfred took place near Ashdown:

The burial place of Baereg, the Danish chief, who was slain in this fight, is distinguished by a parcel of stones, less than a mile from the hill, set on edge, enclosing a piece of ground somewhat raised. On the east side of the southern extremity, stand three squarish flat stones, of about four or five feet over either way, supporting a fourth, and now called by the vulgar Wayland Smith, from an idle tradition about an invisible smith replacing lost horse-shoes there.

A century later Elias Ashmole, who conducted a survey of Berkshire antiquities about 1670 but which was not published until 1719, long after his death in 1692, was brief:

At Ashbury Park, in this Parish [Ashbury] is a Camp of an oblong Figure, about 100 Paces Diameter, and the Works single, which is an Evidence of its Danish Original. It is now almost destroyed, by digging for the Sarseden Stones, to build a House for the Right Honourable Proprietor the Lord Craven.

Construction of the main part of the house, Ashdown House, began about 1663 with two flanking structures added about 1683. The walls are of dressed chalk and Bath stone is used for the quoins and windows. Hundreds of sarsen stones lie in the valley in front of the house, many of which were used to build a wall around the park. Others may have been used for the foundations, but it is most unlikely that stones would have been brought from Wayland's Smithy, there being so many at the site (Plates 16 and 17).

About the same time that Ashmole wrote, John Aubrey, in a survey of antiquities commanded by Charles II conducted largely between the years 1665 and 1693, but not published until 1980-82 having lain in manuscript form all that time in the Bodleian Library at Oxford, also referred to it: 'About a mile from the Hill there are a great many large stones, which though very confused, must yet be laid there on purpose. Some of them are placed edgewise, but the rest are so disorderly, that one would imagine, they were tumbled

Plate 16. The sarsen stones in front of Ashdown House.

out of a cart.' He accompanied it with a sketch of the layout, the first illustration we have and confirming that the site was oblong. Some later antiquaries, after many of the stones had been removed, suggested it was once circular (Fig. 3).

The antiquary Francis Wise explained in 1738 that the disorder was due to people toppling the uprights and breaking them up to mend the highways. His illustration depicts an alleged view from the side, and the structure, not recognisable as Wayland's Smithy, to be in the open. It appears to have been drawn from imagination and the plan copied from Aubrey (Fig. 4). In 1847 it was reported the vault or cave was covered with large stones of which now only one remained, a large quantity having been taken to build a barn towards the end of the eighteenth century. In addition the sarsens were used by people to build walls, the smaller ones being broken by lighting a fire under them and when they

Plate 17. Ashdown House.

were hot throwing water on them, which caused them to split and fall to pieces. Perhaps it was a decline in superstition that led to the destruction of monuments in the eighteenth century, but Wayland's Smithy did not suffer as badly as Avebury (perhaps because of the large numbers of stones at Ashdown) where, as H. J. Massingham records:

> ...eighteenth century Farmer Green, whose execrable zeal heated up the stones, poured cold water over them and then broke them up for haulage, twenty cartloads to a single stone.

20   Myths and Mysteries of Wayland Smith

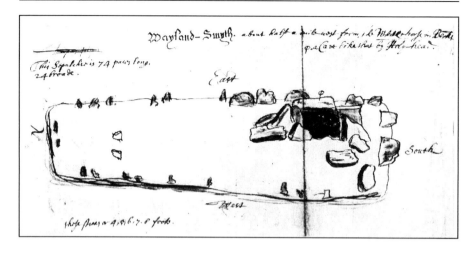

Top: Fig.3. The sketch by John Aubrey, 1670. © The Bodleian Library.
Bottom: Fig.4. The illustration by Francis Wise, 1738.

Opposite: Fig.5. Plan of the site by Lewis, 1868, and the supposed arrangement of the sarsen stones at Ashdown.

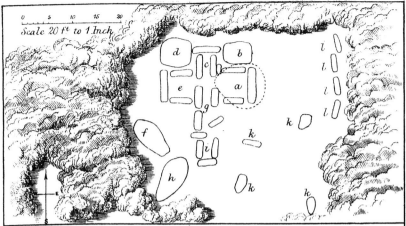

"WAYLAND SMITH'S CAVE", BERKSHIRE.

a, lateral chamber on which the Capstone (marked..........) remains.
b, capstone of gallery chamber c.— d, capstone of chamber e.
f, capstone of gallery g.— h capstone of gallery i.
k.k, detached flat stones.— l.l. upright stones apparently forming part of a circle round the tomb.

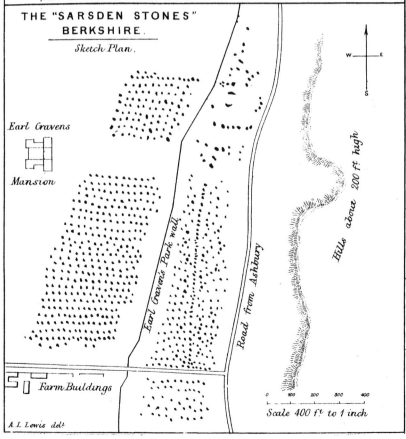

All the king's centuries spent themselves in vain upon the Avebury stones: the triumph was reserved for Messrs. Green and Robinson. A kind of dementia appears to have seized these dull finite clods, and to have directed them towards spending most of their lives in the work of demolition. Many of the stones they broke to pieces, others went to build cow-sheds and pig-sties, pubs and cottages.

Huge sarsen stones or 'grey wethers' – the name 'sarsen' being a corruption of saracen or foreigner (or perhaps from the Celtic *sarn* meaning causeway, i.e. stones used for a causeway) – are boulders of hardened sandstone which once overlay the chalk and now lie scattered on the Downs in this part of the country, especially in Wiltshire. Many have strange legends attached to them. There are those at Ashbury said to be sheep petrified by Merlin, King Arthur's magician. Others call them Druid stones, from a fancied association with Iron Age worshippers. Some local people once believed they grew out of the ground, which in a sense they do, gradually coming to the surface due to weathering away of the topsoil and contraction of the ground in winter frosts.

About two miles south-east of Wayland's Smithy are the 'Sarsden Stones' partly inside and partly outside of Ashdown Park, the low wall of which, of considerable length, appears to be built of fragments of the stones, although they may simply have been stones cleared from the fields to facilitate ploughing. As described by A. L. Lewis in 1868, the stones at one time must have numbered several hundreds, extending over a somewhat irregular parallelogram of about 500 to 600 yards north and south, by 250 to 300 yards east and west, and appear to have been from two to four yards apart. But vast numbers of them had been removed to construct neighbouring roads and buildings, and Lewis noted that when he re-visited the site thirteen months later in 1869, a great number of the smaller stones had gone. The largest stones were about ten feet long, six to nine feet wide, and three to four feet high; but the majority were from two to four feet in length and breadth, and one to three feet in height, many perhaps being fragments of formerly larger stones. Although alleged originally to be arranged in long and somewhat irregular lines (Fig. 5), possibly resembling a network rather than parallel lines, an examination in 1920 deduced they were in a natural position, scattered randomly. In front of the house the stones were cleared away. Between the site and Wayland's Smithy were two or three small stones which Lewis speculated might have been the remains of an avenue leading from one to the other.

One sarsen of particular note 1½ miles east of Whitehorse Hill, although a natural curiosity and not an artefact, is the 'Blowing Stone' or 'King Alfred's Bugle Horn', so called because by someone blowing into a hole in the top it makes a siren-like sound audible up to two or more miles away. It is shown on John Rocque's map of Berkshire of 1761 approximately in its present position. Unknown to Wise, it appears it was probably originally on Whitehorse Hill and moved from there between 1750 and 1760.

Wise continued his description of Wayland's Smithy: 'Those [stones] that are left enclose a piece of ground of an irregular figure at present, but which formerly might have been an oblong square, extending duly North and South.' He added he knew of no other monument of this sort in England but there were several in Wales and Anglesey. From studies in Denmark antiquaries there considered that where there was a single capstone, as appeared to be the case here, it was to be looked upon as a 'Sepulchral Altar, where sacrifices were to be annually performed in honour of the defunct.' But in Denmark three such altars were commonly found together designed, it is supposed, for the service of their three chief deities, Thor, Woden and Frea. Of course our cromlech had three chambers, and doubtless originally three capstones, but this was not evident when Wise wrote.

Wise went on:

Whether this remarkable piece of Antiquity ever bore the name of the person here buried, is not now to be learned; the true meaning of it being long since lost in ignorance and fable. All the account, which the country people are able to give of it, is

'At this place lived formerly an invisible Smith; and if a traveller's Horse had lost a Shoe upon the road, he had no more to do, than to bring the Horse to this place, with a piece of money, and leaving both there for some little time, he might come again and find the money gone, but the Horse new shod'.

Scott claimed Wayland's fee was sixpence (in his story a silver groat), and that 'unlike other workmen' he was offended if more was offered. In 1861 local people said the fee was a penny.

Wise was ignorant of the legend of Wayland, considering that the site was called Wayland's Smithy because it was by the wayside of the Ridgeway, and postulated it must have been the burial place of King Ethelred, killed by the Danes in 871. Aubrey had speculated: 'And this great sepulchre called Wayland Smith is not unlikely to be a great a rude monument of Hengist or Horsa, for in their countrey remaine many monuments like it.'

Another antiquary, the Reverend William Stukeley, toured the south-west in 1724 studying antiquities and producing a book *Itinerarium curiosum*, but overlooked Wayland's Smithy. It was not until 1758 he wrote in his diary for October 3rd:

> My daughter [Anna] Fairchild having been in Barkshire, gave me an account of Whitehorse-hill, and the places thereabouts; the remains of a round temple of the Druids called Wayland Smith... The figure of the horse on the side of the hill is poorly drawn, though of an immense bulk: but, she says, very much in the scheme of the Brittish horses on the reverse of their coins. They found a quantity of gold Brittish coins near there lately, hollow, and like of Cunobeline. Near the white horse, upon the hill, is a large tumulus, which they call pendragon. I believe this hill was one of their places of horse and chariot races at the midsummer sacrifice in the times of the British kings, like that of Black Hameldon in Yorkshire, it being a fine down.

Little wonder Thomas Hearne, the Oxford antiquary and assistant at the Bodleian Library, wrote in 1724:

Fig. 6. Illustration in Lyson's *Magna Britannia*, 1806.

This Dr. S. is a mighty conceited man, and 'tis observed by all that I have talked with that what he does hath no manner of likeness to the original. He goes all by fancy....In short as he addicts himself to fancy altogether what he does must have no regard among judicious and truly ingenious men. He told me he had been at Thame thinking it was a Roman City. Good God! This is nothing but idle dreaming. How is it possible to think at this rate?...Though he be a Physician, yet I am informed he knows very little or nothing of the matter.

Fig.7. Illustration from *The Mirror of Literature, Amusement, and Instruction*, July 1826, "Wayland Smith's Cave", showing fir trees surrounding it.

Fig.8. Illustration from *The Mirror of Literature, Amusement, and Instruction*, February 1833.

An illustration of 1806 in Lyson's *Magna Britannia* shows it to be in the open with no trees around it, more covering stones appeared to be in place and earth seemed to be piled against the central stones (Fig. 6). The writer called it a tumulus, 'over which are, irregularly scattered, several of the large stones, called *Sarsden Stones*, found in

Fig. 9. Illustration of 'Wayland Smith's Cave, probably about 1830.

that neighbourhood; three of the largest have a fourth laid on them in the manner of the British *Cromlechs*. It is most probable that this tumulus is *British*.'

About 1810 the ground covering and surrounding the stones was planted with fir trees and beeches, forming a circular plantation called here a folly, hence Wayland's Folly, a name that did not stick. The planting was after the site had been cleared at the direction of Lord Craven who owned the site, the monument being made considerably more conspicuous. A drawing by 'a Correspondent' in *The Mirror of Literature, Amusement, and Instruction* for 1826, shows the site amongst a stand of fir trees (Fig. 7), but an illustration in the same magazine in 1833 is copied from Francis Wise (Fig. 8). Akerman depicted it in 1847 as surrounded by fir trees and also provided a careful illustration of the layout (Figs. 10 & 11). Professor Donaldson showed it as open the following year but stated that 'some years since' it had been closely planted around with fir-trees (Fig. 12). In 1859, the firs having died were cut down, leaving the exterior ring of beeches. In 1861 it was referred to as in a very neglected state, covered with elder bushes, briars and nettles and when A. L. Lewis visited it in 1868 he referred to it as within a plantation the denseness of which made it difficult to trace the surrounding layout of stones.

Fig.10. One of Akerman's illustrations, 1847.

An illustration in *The Book of Days* for 1888 depicts a double row of mature beech trees in the background but one can not be certain that this illustration, by far the most forbidding-looking, was drawn from observation (Fig. 13). The cave is described thus:

> This now well-known monument of a remote antiquity stands in the parish of Ashbury, on the western boundaries of Berkshire, among the chalkhills which form a continuation of the Wiltshire downs, in a district covered with ancient remains. It is simply a primitive sepulchre, which, though now much dilapidated, has originally consisted of a rather long rectangular apartment, with two lateral chambers, formed by upright stones, and roofed with large slabs. It was, no doubt, originally covered with a mound of earth, which in course of time has been in great part removed. It belongs to a class of monuments

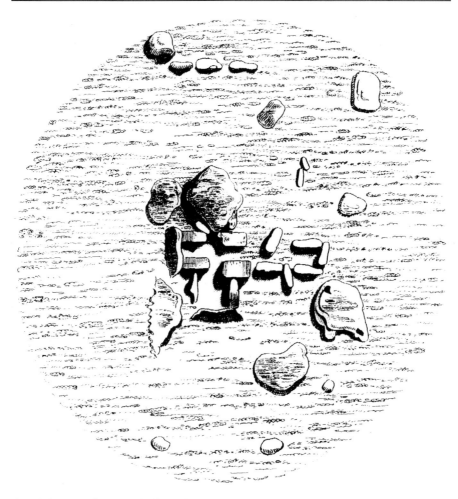

Fig.11. Another of Akerman's illustrations, 1847.

which is usually called Celtic, but, if this be a correct denomination, we must take it, no doubt, as meaning Celtic during the Roman period, for it stands near a Roman road, the Ridgway, which was the position the Romans chose above all others, while the Britons in the earlier period, if they had any highroads at all, which is very doubtful, chose in preference the tops of hills for their burial-place. A number of early sepulchral monuments might be pointed out in different parts of our island, of the same class, and more important than Wayland Smith's Cave, but it has obtained an especial celebrity through two or three circumstances.

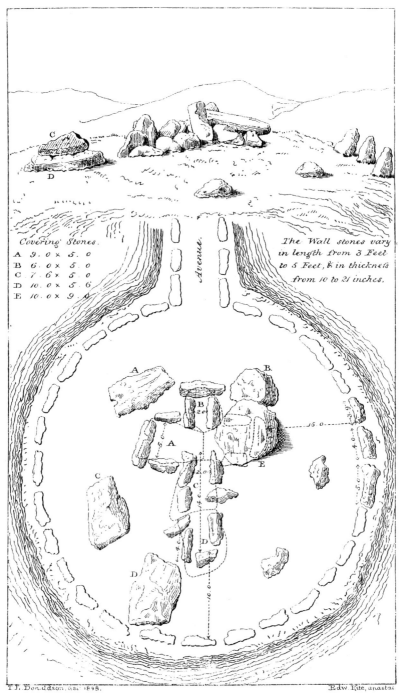

Fig.12. Donaldson's illustrations, 1848.

Fig.13. Illustration in Chamber's *Book of Days*, 1888.

In the first place, this is the only monument of the kind which we find directly named in an Anglo-Saxon document. It happened to be on the line of boundary between two Anglo-Saxon estates, and, therefore, became a marked object. In the deed of conveyance of the estate in which this monument is mentioned, of a date some time previous to the Norman Conquest, it is called Welandes Smiththan, which means Weland's Smithy, or forge, so that its modern name, which is a mere slight corruption from the Anglo-Saxon one, dates itself from a very remote period. In the time of Lysons, to judge from his account of it, it was still known merely by the name of Wayland Smith, so that the further corruption into Wayland Smith's Cave appears to be of very recent date. It is also worthy of remark, that the Anglo-Saxon name appears to prove that in those early times the monument had been already uncovered of its earth, and was no longer recognised as a sepulchral monument, for the Anglo-Saxons would hardly have given the name of a forge, or smithy, to what they knew to be a tomb; so that we have reason for believing that many of our cromlechs and monuments of this description had already been uncovered of their mounds in Anglo-Saxon times. They were probably opened in search of treasure.

But, perhaps the most curious circumstance of all connected with this monument is its legend. It has been the popular belief among the peasantry in modern times, that should it happen to a traveller passing this way that his horse cast a shoe, he had only to take the animal to the 'cave', which they supposed to be inhabited by an invisible, to place a groat on the copestone, and to withdraw to a distance from which he could not see the operation, and on his return, after a short absence, he would find his horse properly shod, and the money taken away. To explain this, it is necessary only to state that, in the primitive Anglo-Saxon and Teutonic mythology, Weland was the mythic smith, the representative of the ancient Vulcan, the Greek Hephaistos.

The article goes on to repeat the legend and continues:

We have found the name, and one of the legends connected with it, fixed in a remote corner of Berkshire, where they have been preserved long after their original import was forgotten. It is one of the most curious examples of the great durability of popular legends of all kinds. We know the whole legend of Weland the smith was perfectly well known to the Anglo-Saxons to a late period of their monarchy.

Other traditions
Several other traditions are associated with the site of which Scott was probably unaware, as he did not use them. One was that a golden coffin was buried nearby, another that an underground passage leads from the cave to a spot near Ashbury, and shepherds and others stated in 1861 that on driving a crowbar into the ground near the 'cave' a very hollow sound was produced. They were

convinced there was a cavity beneath, but underground passages are favourite myths of countryfolk, although usually associated with buildings in villages and towns. Gold coffins are wishful imaginings, although they may have a basis in grave robbing. Alfred Williams, the Swindon railway worker known as the 'hammerman poet', reports 'Strawberry Baxter, the old-time village cobbler' as declaring there was a huge cavern at Wayland's Smith, and a subterranean way which opened in the coombs at Ashbury.

Scott appeared to show a knowledge of the story of Snivelling Corner. In one of the local legends Wayland sent his favourite imp to Ashbury to get some nails. Instead of returning straight back the imp went bird nesting with some of the villagers. Impatiently awaiting, when Wayland saw this he threw a huge boulder at the imp which rolled down the hill and struck him on the heel, causing him to sit down and cry at a spot which is known to this day as Snivelling Corner. Allegedly the heelprint can still be seen in the boulder which lies in the corner of a field of Odstone or Oldstone Farm. Although reported to have disappeared by the archaeologist L. V. Grinsell in 1978, the stone is in fact still there. I could not see any mark resembling a heel, nor have earlier investigators, although there are large oyster-shaped surface fractures more like a giant's heelprint than an imp's, but the weathered sarsen may well have had a heel-like impression on it at one time (Plates 18-19). Alfred Williams suggested that perhaps the heel story derived from the stone originally being known as a *heol* or 'sun'-stone, from *helios*, Greek for sun, referring to a Druidical altar connection. Bayley states that from this stone the midwinter sunrise would appear just over Wayland's Smithy and the summer sunset over the stone from Wayland's Smithy, hence the name heel stone, from *haul*, the Celtic masculine noun for sun. However, although the alignment may be correct, neither is visible the one from the other because Wayland's Smithy is sited well over the brow of the hill.

A slightly different version of the legend was given by villagers in Ashbury and Compton about 1860, namely that Wayland had a

Top: Plate 18. The stone at Snivelling Corner, 1999.
Bottom: Plate 19. The stone at Snivelling Corner, 1999.

servant or apprentice whom he one day sent down the hill for fire to Shrivenham, five miles off. The boy lingered on the way and enraged Wayland, who cast the huge stone at him. And then we have Madame Hughes's version relayed to the Reverend Barham in which Wayland kicked the stone after the imp.

We have no clue as to how the name Snivelling Corner appeared on the first Ordnance Survey map (1818), but it is suggested that the source of the information was the Reverend H. Miller, Vicar of Ashbury. It may simply have derived from the Old English word *snad*, meaning a detached piece of woodland, but Bayley suggests the name may have derived from the Celtic *saer yn efail*, or 'the little artificer of the smithy enclosure's corner'.

No version other than the Berkshire legend refers to Wayland having an assistant, although the concept of the imp comes from the belief in the association of dwarfs with metal workers. In the original Norse legend Wayland was taught his art by two dwarfs. When Mrs. Hughes, who had the story of Snivelling Stone from a servant, first told it to Scott, he declared he had never heard of Wayland having had any attendant, relying solely on Camden for his information. His creation of Dickie Sludge, a character so near the traditional one of which he had never heard, was a curious coincidence. It was Scott who named the imp Flibbertigibbet, a name which does not occur in the original legends but is now repeated as folklore. Flibbertigibbet was a sixteenth-century name for a gossipy woman, although Shakespeare in *King Lear* applied it to a fiend. In the folklore of eighteenth-century southern Norway, and probably earlier, Madame Flappetylappet, so called on account of her long tail, was a kind of witch who led the wild host of the wicked dead who were condemned to ride about until the end of the world. Christmas was their favourite time of the year for showing themselves. In nineteenth-century Berkshire dialect, flibberty-gibberty meant flighty or unreliable.

A shepherd of Uffington, Job Cork, who wrote rhymes about the end of the 18th century, dying in 1807 at the age of 67, wrote:

If you along the Rudgeway go,
About a mile for aught I know,
There Wayland's cave then you may see,
Surrounded by a group of trees.

They say that in this cave did dwell
A smith that was invisible;
At last he was found out, they say,
He blew up the place and vlod away.

To Devonshire then he did go,
Full of sorrow, grief and woe,
Never to return again;
So here I'll add the shepherd's name -
Job Cork.

Written well before Scott's version in Kenilworth, this poem could have been relayed to Scott by Mrs. Hughes. If not it provides another curious coincidence, for although Scott refers to Devonshire and the blowing-up of the cave, the reference to Devonshire has no known connection with the Wayland Smith legend, nor does blowing-up the cave occur in the legends. We are left wondering whether in fact Scott did not have some prior knowledge of the local legends which he had completely forgotten about when he stated that he obtained all of his information from Camden.

Job Cork's poem also indicates the site had trees around it before those planted by Lord Craven in 1810. Nothing is known of Job Cork or if he wrote any other poems. Parish records show a Job Corke to have married Mary Davis at Uffington in October 1735 and who therefore would have been in his nineties when he died – if he was the poet – and a Job Corke to have been christened in March 1772, son of Job and Elizabeth, who would have been 35 in 1807. But his father, whose birth, marriage and death are unrecorded, at least in Berkshire, although he was apparently born in 1740, could have been the poet in question.

Because of the myth of the capstones being used originally as

Plate 20. The witches moon dial with, inset, a sketch of the markings. The base is added for display.

sacrificial altars, satanist services are apparently held at Wayland's Smithy, possibly on an annual basis and dating back perhaps two or three hundred years. In October 1998 the tiny thirteenth-century church of St. Swithun's in Compton Beauchamp was broken into and the tabernacle smashed. The churchwarden believed the robbers were trying to steal the chalice and sacraments to use at Wayland's Smithy. In 1939 an object about 8 inches high and 5 inches across, referred to as a 'Witches' Moon-dial' used on moonlight nights, apparently made of human bone with seven inscribed marks representing the 'Seven Hours of Dread', was allegedly found near Wayland's Smithy (Plate 20). In the same year bought in a curiosity shop was a human skull marked 'Wayland's Smithy' accompanied by a piece of paper stating it was at one time in the possession of 'Mary Chalmers, a woman of skill in the curing of cows and sheep, who died on June 4th 1810, and lived at Little Moreton', east of Didcot.

A century after Wise introduced the idea of a sacrificial function for the capstone the idea that the slabs were used as sacrificial altars was generally rejected, although Professor Donaldson still favoured the idea in 1848: 'perhaps the covering of stones themselves served as altars, and on them were possibly offered the human victims, sacrificed to propitiate the manes of the dead, or to appease by their bloody rites the wrath of the savage gods of the Druid Priests.' His contemporary Thurnam considered the broken and burnt bones found in some barrows signified cannibal feasts held at the burial when slaves, captives, wives and concubines of the dead lord were sacrificed and then eaten. In his book *Downland Man*, the archaeologist H. J. Massingham wryly remarked that the writer Grant Allen, whose imagination seemingly knew no bounds, 'had apparently been reading Dr. Thurnam to the detriment of his night's sleep' when he wrote the following description of a long barrow burial:

> I saw them bear aloft, with beating breasts and loud gesticulations, the bent corpse of their dead chieftain: I saw the terrified and fainting wives haled along by thongs of raw ox-hide, and the weeping prisoners driven passively like sheep to the slaughter: I saw the fearful orgy of massacre and rapine around the open tumulus, the wild priest shattering with his gleaming tomahawk the skulls of his victims, the fire of gorse and low brushwood prepared to roast them, the heads and feet flung carelessly on the top of the yet uncovered stone chamber, the awful dance of blood-stained cannibals around the mangled

remains of men and oxen, and, finally, the long task of heaping up above the stone hut of the dead king the earthen mound that was never again to be opened to the light of day, til, ten thousand years later, we modern Britons invaded with our prying, sacriligeous mattock the sacred privacy of the cannibal ghost.

The title of the book? *Falling in Love!*

Massingham argued human sacrifice was not introduced until the middle and late Bronze Ages and is not generally found associated with long barrows. People in the Neolithic Age he saw as peaceful, they could not have built their gigantic long barrows and 'hill forts' (believed to be gathering centres for ritual and trade and not defensive positions) if they were under threat of war, for they took a long time to build and occupied many people in their construction. The low population density in Neolithic times perhaps meant there was ample land for everyone and so people had no need to fight one another.

In Yorkshire, perhaps coming from Scandinavian sources rather than Saxon, part of the myth of Wayland Smith is enshrined in reference to Wayland's mythical grandfather, the giant Wade. Local legend has him residing at Mulgrave Castle and building the Roman road which runs near to it called Wade's Causeway. The remains of a cromlech in the form of two large stones in the neighbourhood are called Wade's Grave. John Leland, antiquary of Henry VIII, touring England and Wales from 1536 to 1542 in search of material (he overlooked Wayland Smith) wrote that at Mulgrave there were '…certen Stones communely caullid Waddes Grave, whom the People there say to have bene a Gigant and owner of Mougreve.' An English romance of Wade referred to by Chaucer is irretrievably lost.

Fragments of a carved cross dating from about 1000 in the church of St. Peter, Leeds , in the West Riding of Yorkshire, bear a lower panel which has been interpreted as Wayland wearing wings and seizing a valkyrie, a hammer and tongs being shown in the corner. The cross also apprently depicts a scene from the Siegfried saga. A Northumbrian carved cross of the 10th to 11th century from Halton in Lancashire, also seemingly illustrates a scene of Wayland before an anvil raising a large hammer, with above it tongs and a headless person; and also a scene from the Siegfrid saga. Bearing similar carvings, the island of Gotland in Sweden has a number of carved 'picture stones' of peculiar 'mushroom' shape in flat outline with versions of the Wayland and Siegfrid legends. One at Tjängvide shows Odin's eight-legged horse Sleipnir, while another from Ardre church depicts Wayland with a hammer and tongs and two headless bodies.

Always Wayland is depicted as someone taking his fearful revenge.

In Norfolk there is the Hundred of Wayland in which is Wayland's Wood, but its town of Watton, interpreted as Wat's or Wade's town, could simply refer to a man named Wada. An Anglo-Saxon Charter of 903 concerning a grant of land at Risborough in Buckinghamshire, has a note on the back of a later copy referring to a landmark *Welandes stocc*, meaning Wayland's stump or tree trunk. In Somerset there was a Wayland's Pond and a garbled tale of a smith who once shod the devil's horse.

2
Wayland's Smithy

Where the great grey Stones from out the earth
stand up so stark and drear.

Buck, 1928.

'Then the people...wrought a mound' (Beowulf)
Long barrows of the Neolithic Age and round barrows of the Bronze Age are common in Berkshire and Wiltshire on and near the Downs, the great high chalk ridge which runs from east to west for 85 miles from Wiltshire to Buckinghamshire, surmounted by its ancient road the Ridgeway, or Rudgeway as old Berkshire people called it. The oblong tumulus with chambers confined to its eastern or southern end, appears peculiar to Somerset, Wiltshire, Gloucestershire and Berkshire (Oxfordshire), corresponding more closely with the 'Giants Chamber' in Northern Ireland than with the so-called 'Cromlechs' of Denmark.

Prominent among these memorials, Wayland's Smithy was built by people of the Early Neolithic (or Early New Stone Age) in the middle of the 4th millennium BC, sometime between 3700 and 3400 BC, on top of an already existing burial mound. The 'new mound' is the oldest in the area, pre-dating more dramatic structures such as Stonehenge. The site appears to be in isolation from contemporary monuments and settlements, and there is little evidence of flint working around the site or of its use. Most earlier Neolithic flint working appears three kilometres to the south around Weathercock Hill, but there are at least four ring ditches to the immediate west and one a little to the east, evidence of some adjacent settlement (Plate 22). A few fragments do however suggest a possible New

Plate 21. View from the air, 2000. © English Heritage. NMR.

Stone Age camp on the site, and there are hints it may have already been used for special transactions: a high-quality ground axe of Cornish stone, a deliberately broken flint axe, and fragments of three types of pottery. The broken flint axe was found on the surface under the original barrow, placed or discarded there before the barrow was erected. The broken portions of ground stone axe were found in the filling of one of the first ditches dug to provide the rubble to cover the tomb.

This first structure was developed over a period of time, not constructed as a 'one-off' as a post-battle burial would imply. Excavations in 1919, confirmed in 1962-3, revealed an earlier mound of chalk covering a cairn about midway along the present visible mound, the smallest 'unchambered' long barrow hitherto discovered in Britain, 'unchambered' in that the chambers were not

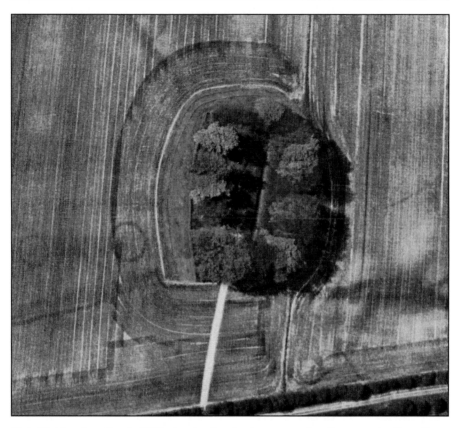

Plate 22. View from the air, 1976, showing the circular crop marks of iron-age dwellings, the ancient line of the Ridgeway, and the track to the north-west. © Crown copyright. NMR.

constructed of stone and could not be re-opened for further burials once covered by a mound. Its maximum length and breadth were fifty-four and twenty-seven feet respectively, and its original height likely to have been at least six feet. The outline of the mound was markedly irregular, but then the smooth contours of intact mounds that we see today may have as much to do with weathering and surface erosion as they have with being constructed by primitive artisans. The outline of the mound had originally been marked by small sarsen slabs up to three feet in height, most of which had probably already been dug out during the first thousand years BC as they obstructed ploughing. They were not set in holes but leant against the mound. The mound itself consisted of a basal cairn of sarsen boulders averaging one foot in diameter, covered with clean chalk rubble derived from ditches dug either side for this purpose. A kerb

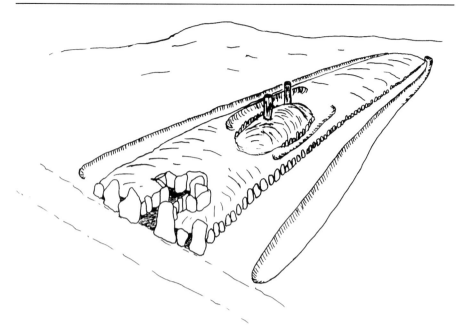

Fig.14. Artist's impression of the second barrow under construction. The first barrow is shown covered over with the tree trunks left in place. In the second the capstones are not in place.

of sarsen stones kept the chalk from sliding back into the ditches from which it had been excavated. It is believed the boulders would have been gathered into piles during cultivation of the adjacent downland. Under the cairn was a pavement of flat sarsen stones sixteen feet long by five feet wide, laid on bare chalk, the turf having first been stripped off, flanked by two banks of small sarsen boulders up to a height of two feet. At each end of the pavement a massive four-feet diameter split tree trunk had been erected. These half tree-trunks apparently reached well above the surface of the mound (Fig. 14).

At least fourteen bodies, but it could have been seventeen or more, had been deposited on the pavement in different states of decay from nearly complete articulation to complete disarticulation. There were more than twice as many male as female. Nine or ten were young adults, and one a child of about nine years old. A further three or four adults were represented by skulls and fragments only. Considered similar at the time to local people in their bone structure, the men were about five-and-a-half feet in height, one almost six feet, and the women were of similar height to the men.

A large proportion of the smaller bones was found to be missing, particularly the hands, feet, knee-caps and lower jaws, while only a minute fraction had been gnawed by rodents. The conclusion drawn from this was that the bodies must have been exposed after death on a platform where parts were removed by carrion-eating birds. This could have been to allow their spirits to ascend into the heavens, perhaps the idea being that the birds would take them there, otherwise the bodies could have been covered. Or perhaps, and more probable in my view, it was an attempt to mummify the bodies by drying in the wind, but the atmosphere being too humid when the bodies were partially decomposed they were taken down and interred.

The only grave goods found were three leaf-shaped flint arrowheads with broken tips, and two with broken butts also. Perhaps they had been deliberately broken to signify the owners would no longer need to hunt, although if there was a belief in afterlife they would have still needed them. Each was in contact with a pelvis and it is possible on the contrary they may have been lodged in the bodies. Arrow heads have been found lodged in skeletons in other barrows. But as there is no evidence that the place was a living site, it is unlikely this was a family group overcome in an attack. Nor was it a place where they laid warriors or chiefs to rest, unless the females and juveniles were slaughtered to be buried with the chief, a not uncommon practice in some primitive societies. But the indications of successive burials do not support this.

There was an empty space on the pavement at the south end, and a single body at the north end separate from the mass of remains. This suggests perhaps they added bodies at the ends, pushing the existing remains further in when the time came to inter another.

It is suggested a ridgepole was supported between the two massive uprights and a wooden tent-like structure covered the bodies. This was later covered with earth and eventually the wooden structure collapsed. Others believe it was a box-like structure of cairns either side with large standing posts at either end, and there was a flat wooden roof or lid resting on the cairns. It is also suggested the site

Fig. 15. Artist's impression of the mummification platform.

might perhaps have first been marked by the massive half-tree trunks which were perhaps carved or crudely painted, forming a landmark for a shrine or some other ritual site, and burial followed later. It is certain the tree trunks were erected before the stone pavement was laid. However, if the remains had not somehow been isolated, not being covered after interment, then bears, wolves, foxes and rats would have attacked and removed the remains.

The most likely arrangement to my mind is that the half-tree trunks supported a platform on which the bodies were placed in order to attempt to dry them in a simple form of mummification. Beneath this was the barrow with the top probably covered with a flat lid made of poles (Fig. 15). Archaeologists ignore the presence of bears, widespread in Britain at this time and not becoming extinct until a thousand years ago. The supporting poles of the platform would have had to be massive enough to withstand bears trying to pull them over, and tall enough to make it difficult for the bears to climb.

So we have an initial Early New Stone Age clearance of the area followed by some use of it. The posts are erected at a later date, supporting the platform beneath which is the mortuary structure, which is in use for some time before it is covered with chalk dug from either side leaving ditches. The area becomes overgrown but is then burnt off about 3700 BC for construction of another barrow. But now ideas have evolved and massive stones are brought to the site to build a tomb, Wayland's Smithy.

'He gazed on the work of giants, saw how the eternal earth building held within stone arches, firm fixed by pillars' (*Beowulf*)

The massive façade of sarsen stones which confronts the visitor to the spot introduces a second, and larger, of two barrows which make up the mound. Not more than 50 years after the first barrow was covered up, a long mound with two sarsen stone-lined chambers off an entrance passage was built over the first barrow. Before building began the site was apparently cleared of vegetation by fire, a burnt branch or trunk permitting radio-carbon dating. Bayley states that seven years was the reign of a sacred Celtic king, thus perhaps the new barrow was built after seven reigns of seven years.

Wayland's Smithy, with a central passage and terminal chamber flanked by a chamber either side to form the shape of a cross, belongs to a wider Cotswold-Severn type of terminally chambered tombs and a type with transepted chambers, that is side chambers, although an outlier of the main area of such tombs. The cruciform plan is uncommon in the region as is the north-south orientation, but the latter may have been dictated by the axis of the original barrow, which presumably showed that at that period an east-west orientation was not important. Although the form of the Latin cross originally aroused some speculation it was generally played down. The side chambers could have been subsequent additions and the reason for their being opposite to each other was because they were larger than the central one and required to be enclosed in that part of the barrow where they would be most covered with earth. In a mound of comparatively small dimensions the centre would present the only favourable position. Suffice to say it is not a higgledy-piggledy arrangement of burial places as we might be tempted to suppose an ignorant savage would have constructed almost 6,000 years ago, but a carefully thought out and measured arrangement (Fig. 16).

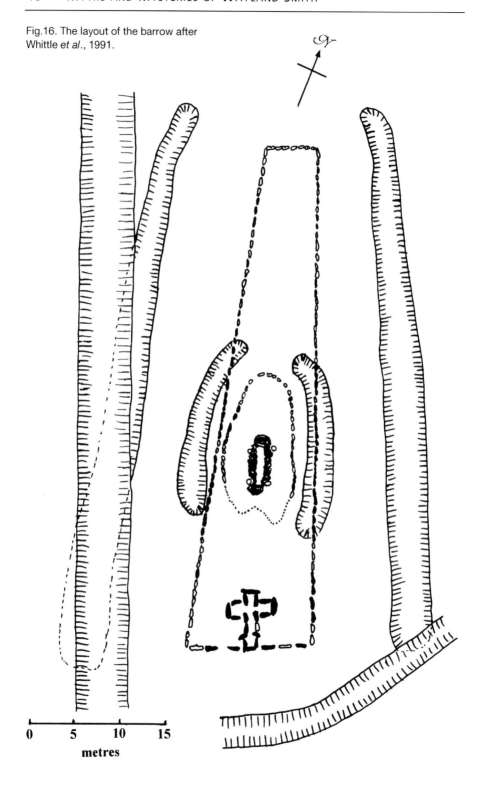

Fig.16. The layout of the barrow after Whittle *et al.*, 1991.

Again using chalk rubble, the covering mound was trapezoidal in shape, 180 feet long and tapering in width from 48 to 20 feet from the entrance to the northern end. The sides and back had been marked by a continuous line of sarsen slabs set against the margins of the mound. To the north all the stones had been removed but at the sides they had become buried. At the south end the mound terminated in a straight façade of six very large sarsens up to ten feet high, either side of the entrance to the chamber. Two are missing. It has been suggested the somewhat pear-shaped outline of the main stones is, as in the Avebury Avenue, meant to represent the shape of a woman. The spaces between the uprights were filled with dry walling. Entering, there is a small antechamber six feet in height. The spaces between the slabs were here filled with dry-stone walling of coral ragstone from at least six kilometres away in the Vale. Perhaps this was a primitive form of gift for the funeral rites, but at least it indicates there was contact with the Vale below.

Apparently a primary barrow, a chambered long barrow, the 'cave' was the eastern burial chamber, the only one surviving surmounted by a coverstone. It is little short of miraculous that this coverstone, of possibly an original eight, was still in position after nearly 6,000 years. It was a rather low mound in the 1930s, oval in shape but probably originally rectangular. At the south-east end was a heap of stones which looked, as Aubrey wrote, as if they had been 'tumbled out of a cart'. But most were standing upright arranged in the form of a cross. The long arm of the cross is really a long passage which led to the remains of three burial chambers forming the shorter arms of the cross, where some skeletons were found in 1919. It is thus a monument comprising a long barrow of the true passage-grave type with an entrance and passage leading to burial chambers, one of which still had its capstone in place. The inner surfaces of some of the stones seem to be smoother than the outer, having been carefully worked, particularly the inner faces of the eastern chamber. Erecting the façade of great sarsen stones is estimated to have required 35 to 50 able-bodied men.

What makes this site of such importance is that it appears to demonstrate a change in funerary practice from attempts at mummification to simple entombment. So were the builders of this barrow new arrivals who brought with them belief in the afterlife and the custom of mummification from pharaonic Egypt, or had these beliefs been slowly penetrating across Europe from Egypt, and had these peoples been gradually advancing inland from the coast trying to find a suitable place where they could exercise their religious beliefs? The importance is that here, on this very spot, a change in practices took place. Finding mummification unsuccessful even here with its high winds, they took to copying the tombs of Ancient Egypt, the chambered style known as the *mastaba*, all in the space of some fifty years.

It was in the early part of the twentieth century that Dr. Elliot Smith proposed that the design of the chambered long barrow was derived from the Ancient Egyptian *mastaba*-tomb of the earlier dynasties, a concept taken up by a number of authorities, although others thought too much stress was being laid upon an Egyptian influence. Were the barrows the local equivalent of the pyramids of Egypt which were being constructed contemporaneously, the people doing the best they could with the materials available to them? If so, did the knowledge diffuse outwards from Egypt through the meeting of trade routes? But this was no simple adoption of traders' tales of the wonders of Egypt, but a whole culture of belief, a belief in the afterlife and the necessity of mummification. This was a culture brought to the Downs, not developed there, and the only known origin was Egypt. And harking back to the legend of Wayland Smith, which I pointed out may have had its origins in the Middle East in Mycenean times, it could have come to the Berkshire Downs with the tomb builders, not after them.

Early descriptions

Aubrey showed in 1670 that the stones by which the tumulus was surrounded had an oval or oblong and not a circular arrangement. He states the 'sepulchre' was 74 paces long and 24 broad. Wise described the cave in 1738 as on the east side of the southern extremity 'of the enclosed piece of ground raised a few feet above the common level', consisting of 'three squarish flat stones of about four or five feet over each way, set on edge, and supporting a Fourth of much larger dimensions, lying flat upon them. These altogether form a Cavern or sheltring place, resembling pretty exactly those described by Wormius, Bartholine, and others, except in the dimensions of the stones; for whereas this may shelter only ten or a dozen sheep from a storm, Wormius mentions one in Denmark, that would shelter a hundred.'

'There seem to have been two approaches to our Altar through rows of large stones set on edge, one from the South, the other from the West, the latter leading directly into the Cavern.' Wises's western approach was really the side chamber.

Sir Richard Hoare, who referred to it as 'a ridiculous name given to a British monument of very high antiquity', described it in 1821 as 'a long barrow, having a kistvaen of stones within it, to protect the place of interment. A line of stones encircled the head of the barrow, of which I noticed four standing in their original position; the corresponding four on the opposite side had been displaced... The long barrows almost invariably point towards the east, at which end is found the sepulchral deposit, but this barrow deviates from the general rule, by pointing north and south. The adit or avenue, the stones of which still remain, goes straight from south to north, then turns abruptly to the east, where we find the kistvaen, covered by the large incumbent stone, which measures ten feet by nine.'

But it is in fact much more than a kistvaen, which is a degenerate cist, or nothing more than a small cairn of stones heaped on the remains of the dead and covered by a mound.

The fact that the barrow and gallery leading to the chambers pointed to the south, rather than east, may have been in consequence of the position of the Ridgeway in that direction.

It was described thus in 1848 by Professor Donaldson:

> The central figure has the form of a Latin Cross, the whole length being some 22 or 23 feet from out to out; its greatest

width is 15 feet. Each end of the four arms of the Cross is closed by a larger sized stone from 5 to 7 feet long and 15 to 24 inches thick, the longer arm answering to the nave of a church is 2 feet wide inside and 14 feet long, having now on one side four blocks, and on the other three; but I am inclined to think one has been displaced, and that there were four on that side also. These stones forming the walls are 14 or 15 in number, and vary from 3 feet long to 4 feet. The shorter arms of transepts are about 5 feet wide, and they are 5 feet deep, thus presenting the appearance of chambers 5 feet square, with the entrances narrowed to 2 or 3 feet. The short arm at the further end is 4 feet 9 inches to 2 or 3 feet. The short arm at the further end is 4 feet 9 inches deep by 2 feet wide, and is formed by a stone on each side and one at the end.

There were five large blocks to form the roof: one now remains in its place covering the east transept; it is of circular form 10 feet by 9 feet on the surface, and 12 inches thick; it therefore weighs from 5 to 6 tons [now calculated at 4 tons]. The covering block of the other arm or transept is 9 feet long by 5 feet wide: that at the further end 6 feet by 5 feet; the two, which covered the nave, respectively 7 feet 6 inches by 5 feet wide, and 10 feet long by 5 feet wide, and of the same average thickness.

At the distance of 15 feet from the end of the eastern transept are three stones in their places, corresponding in size with the wall stones of the centre group, and varying from 3 feet 9 inches to 5 feet long. They seem to form the arc or portion of a circular outside ring. Although there are only two or three other stones of this size to be found on the site, I am led to think that these three stones formed part of an enclosure, and that the rest have been removed by peasants. The general arrangement then…would present a mound about 50 feet in diameter at the top, surrounded by an outer ditch; the top of this mound having a circle of stones, in the centre of which is a cruciform chamber in the shape of a Latin Cross, there being one arm to the south decidely longer than the others. ...opposite the north end, it appeared...as though there was a continuous embankment, calculated for an alley of stones, or a dromos, as at Avebury.

Lewis in 1868 thought the arrangement of the stones was circular.

Not used for the interment of a single great chief as many old antiquaries liked to imagine, a barrow was used for several generations of burials, and when the last of the great sarsen stones and the capstone were put in place the chambers were sealed.

When the chambers were excavated in 1920 they found the much disturbed remains of perhaps eight skeletons, including a newborn baby, without grave goods. The thigh bones were missing, possibly removed during use of the tomb. After the last interment the chambers were filled with chalk rubble and the passage closed. The area was then apparently abandoned.

Changes with time

Martin Palmer has advanced the theory that originally the burial sites (both here and elsewhere) were unsealed because the skulls were used in ancestor worship, being taken out at certain times to be used in religious rites. But the intense industry of the people exhausted the land causing an ecological crisis, and the faith of the people in the beneficence of their ancestors was destroyed. Prayers to them did not make their crops grow. So they sealed up the tombs once and for all and that was the end of ancestor worship. But at Wayland's Smithy this does not fit in with the sealing of the first tomb, and then the construction and later sealing of the second, grander structure. Unless we postulate that the process of faith abandonment happened twice.

The study of snail shells left in post holes and of those in the buried soil, show that the area was open grassland or farmland but did revert to scrub and woodland soon after the barrows were sealed. The area was then cultivated again in the early Iron Age, when even the sides of the barrow were ploughed, continuing into the Romano-British period. At one stage, probably during the first half of the Iron Age, a ditch was excavated along the western side of the barrow to form a bank between it and the barrow. It is generally considered that ditches may have been dug in the Iron Age to mark field or territorial boundaries, but we cannot rule out the possibility that those here were perhaps for some kind of defensive position. Pottery sherds buried during the construction are of a type found at Uffington Castle and Rams Hill. Later the area between the trench and the barrow was ploughed. In the 1920 study an isolated burial was found on the margin of the field thus formed, outside of the barrow. Perhaps a casualty of a battle. It is undated and could be Early Neolithic, but may be Roman.

During the Romano-British period the trench was recut and a new, shallow one cut across the south-west corner, again suggestive of defence positions although present-day thinking is to regard such ditches as delimiting fields or boundaries. But this south-west trench would cover the Ridgeway, the original western trench would cover any attack from the west, while the defender's eastern side would have been covered by the barrow. To the north, a little removed from the site, was another ditch slanting east-west.

Later, part of the south-west trench was refilled with sarsen boulders amongst which fragments of human bone suggest the tomb chamber was being looted. Two small complementary bronze objects of the eighth century BC suggest possibly a harness fitting and that grave looting may have begun then. When we refer to 'looting', curiosity would be a more apt word, for there could have been nothing of value in the graves. Later in the Roman period cultivation extended over the whole surroundings of the barrow and the northern part of the mound, and the virtual absence of post-Roman pottery sherds suggests denudation of the barrow could have been already largely effected in Roman times, but some consider it may not have been done until the seventeenth or eighteenth centuries. The latter is unlikely in view of the name given to it in the tenth century.

The 'currency bars'

Two iron bars thought to be currency bars of the Celtic period were unearthed near the foot of the fallen western entrance stone in 1919. Their manner of finding suggested they were placed on the ground at the inside of the entrance to the chamber, which meant that the barrow must have already been denuded. Did this indicate a Celtic association of the tradition of the Smith, or the derivation of the tradition? Was Wayland an Iron Age god? The bars were of too late a date to be grave goods and thought to be of a type described by Julius Ceasar in 54 BC, weighing 11 to 12 ounces, 16 to 17 inches long, flat with an expanded end bearing a pair of small holes, presumably for stringing them on a leathern thong.

This is what the discoverer R. A. Smith had to say:

> ...opposite the foot of the slab immediately west of the entrance, two flat rods of iron were taken out together. They were lying parallel to the foot of the jamb, 1 ft. From the present surface, and looked like door-hinges, but the only perforations are in the expanded end of each, and another interpretation was needed. Though a novel variety of the type, they are evidently currency-bars of Early British origin, such as Julius Ceasar described, and no doubt saw during his invasions in B.C. 55-54... The discovery of currency on the site inevitably leads to speculation... In other words, the find of currency-bars not only points to a British predecessor of Wayland, but indicates that although this particular jamb was still standing, the long barrow had been already denuded to its present level in the first century before Christ.

Although they passed into the literature as 'currency bars' and the story still persists, re-examination in 1939 in the research laboratory of the British Museum showed them to be nothing more than blacksmith's ironwork of the eighteenth century or later, and considered to be two halves of a single object of which the narrow ends had been united in a forged joint. The most probable explanation as to

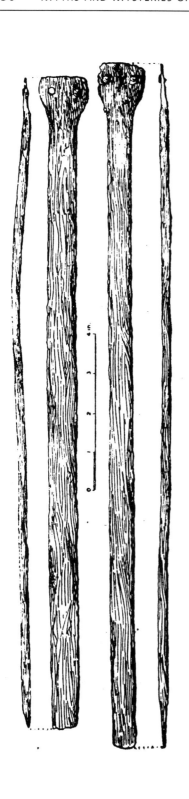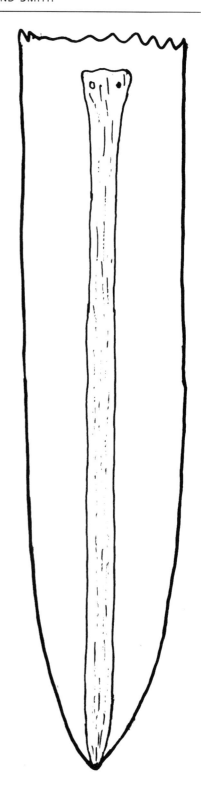

how they got there, to my mind, is they were the reinforcements of the end of a pole used to try and prise out the stones, and the end broke off a foot underground (Fig. 17). Perhaps lucky for us, otherwise these remaining great stones may have been levered out and smashed up.

Opposite: Fig.17. The 'currency bars' as drawn by Smith in 1920. On the right, their probable mode of use as reinforcement to the point of a stake.

3
Origins of the Wayland Smith Legend

'Where are now the bones of the wise Weland?'

Alfred

How does this grim creature of Wayland Smith come to be associated with this lonely spot on the Downs? For grim he certainly was, as blackened by soot and hamstrung to prevent his walking, the mythical smith laboured incessantly at his anvil. The legend is remarkable because it can be traced through its various transformations almost from its origin and in its spread throughout Europe. But the difference between the story of Wayland and other legends in the heroic literature of antiquity is that the hero is clearly represented as a smith, and that cruelty, treachery and vindictiveness are ascribed to the chief characters. The humble workman in the form of the smith is given credit as the essential furnisher of the means by which battles may be won, while at the same time the kings and nobles who have to exercise their bravery with his weapons depend upon him and resent him for such dependence.

It all began with the fall of Vulcan in Ancient Greek mythology.

Myths of Ancient Greece

There are many legends of Vulcan in many countries. Thus Cicero came to the conclusion that one lived in Attica, another in Egypt, a third at Lemnos, and a fourth in the Vulcanian islands near Sicily. All these referred of course to Wayland. A Grecian legend quoted by a lost writer Pytheas of the fourth century BC bears great resemblance to our legend:

> Hephæstus or Vulcan appears to have taken up his abode in the islands of Lipara and Strongyle... it was formerly said, that whoever chose to carry there a piece of unwrought iron, and at the same time deposited the value of the labour, might on the following morning come and have a sword, or whatever else he wished for it.

In Greek mythology he is referred to both as Vulcan and as Hephæstus, inhabiting the Vulcan islands in Sicily. Son of Jupiter and Juno, god of fire and the forge, he was hurled out of heaven by Jupiter and falling for one day and one night landed on top of Mount Mosychlus on the Island of Lemnos in the Aegean Sea. In his fall he injured a leg which left him lamed and deformed. He withdrew to Mount Etna where he established a great forge in the heart of the mountain in partnership with the Cyclopes, the three children of Uranus and Gæa. Named Brontes (Thunder), Steropes (Lightning) and Arges (Sheet-lightning), the three were formerly makers of thunderbolts. They helped Vulcan manufacture many objects in metal. Eventually restored to favour with his father on Mount Olmypus, Vulcan nevertheless returned to his forge and with the aid of the Cyclopes manufactured Jupiter's weapons, thunderbolts, and Cupid's love-inspiring arrows, among other miraculous objects.

Vulcan then fell in love with the goddess Minerva, Goddess of Beauty. She contemptuously dismissed the extremely ugly and sooty Vulcan, so his father Jupiter bestowed upon him the hand of Venus, and sent her with her train of Loves and Graces to reside in the caves of Etna. After a time she left her husband and he married one of the Graces, who also soon tired of him. He is then believed to have had a liaison with the gorgon Medusa, producing several monsters: Cacus, a loathsome giant later slain by Hercules; Periphetes, a giant who stood in the road and with a huge club attacked any who tried to pass, usually killing them, but was eventually slain by Theseus; Cercyon the wrestler, the world-renowned robber, also slain by Theseus; and others.

Vulcan was worshipped by all blacksmiths and artisans who recognized him as their special patron, holding great festivals, the Vulcanalia and the Hephæstia. From this lame smith working in the depths of a cavern, the story of Wayland the Smith in its many forms seems to have emerged and spread across Europe. And in the story of the escape of Volund we also find a perhaps tenuous influence of the story of Dædalus.

Just as the name Wayland derives from the Icelandic word for a smith, Voelundr, so the name Dædalus derived from a Greek word meaning cunningly wrought. The name was given to a mythical far-famed architect who was guilty of the murder of Talus, his sister's son, who promised to rival him in skill. Fleeing Greece he took refuge in Crete and entered into the service of King Minos. Poseidon, god of the sea, sent to Minos a snow-white bull for sacrifice, but instead Minos kept it alive. So Poseidon made the Queen Pasiphæ fall in love with it, and with the help of Daedalus she disguised herself as a cow and her liaison with the bull produced the bull with a man's head known as the Minotaur. Daedalus then constructed a labyrinth in which to hide it but made it so intricate that, together with his son Icarus, he could not find the way out. He then manufactured a pair of wings of feathers stuck to a frame with wax, one each for himself and his son, and by means of this they both escaped. But Icarus ignored his father's warning and flew too high, the sun melted the wax and he sank down into the sea and was drowned. Daedalus escaped to Sicily and we hear no more of him.

The Anglo-Saxon heritage

From these Grecian myths we leap to the Saxons who brought their ancient Teutonic folklore to Britain, for the most ancient references to Wayland are in remains of Anglo-Saxon poetry, in which allusions to the wonders of Wayland's art were very popular. In Beowulf, of the seventh or eighth century, the hero's favourite breast-plate was made by Weland: 'Send to Hygelac, if battle takes me off, the best of battle garments that arms my breast, the finest corslets. That is a heritage from Hrethel, the work of Weland.' In a poem of very early date titled *Deor*, probably written down in the seventh century but dating from the fourth to the sixth, the lament of a minstrel supplanted in his lord's favour by a rival singer seeks comfort by recalling 'old, unhappy, far-off things':

> *Weland the resolute warrior,*
> *had knowledge of exile;*
> *he suffered hardships,*
> *sorrow and longing he had for companions,*
> *wintry cold exile.*
> *Often he found woes*
> *after Nithhad had constrained him,*
> *supple bonds of sinew*
> *upon a more excellent man.*
> *That passed away,*
> *so may this.*

That this lament refers to him only being bound is considered evidence that it antedated the Scandinavian version, the *Edda*, where binding was not cruel enough and they had him hamstrung instead.

The minstrel continues with other parts of the story found in the *Edda* showing the legends to be identical.

King Alfred, translating Boethius's *De Consolatione Philosophiae* in the ninth century, inserts: 'What are now the bones of the celebrated, and the wise goldsmith, Weland? I have therefore said the wise, because to the skilful his skill can never be lost, nor can any man more easily take it from him, than he can move the sun from her place. Where are now the bones of Weland; or who knows now where they were?' rendering the lines

'Ubi nunc fidelis ossa Fabricii manent?',
instead of as Fabricius, a proper name, as *faber*, a smith or artisan: 'Where are now the bones of Weland; or who knows now where they were?' Later this was turned into a metrical version:

> *Where are now the bones of the wise Weland,*
> *the goldsmith,*
> *who was formerly most famous?'*
> *Who knows now the bones*
> *of the wise Weland,*
> *under what mound*
> *they are concealed?*

Boethius actually wrote:

> *…Death despises the heights of glory,*
> *Enfolds alike the humble and the proud,*
> *Making the lowest equal to the highest.*
> *Where are now the bones of good Fabricius?*
> *What is Brutus now, or stern old Cato?*
> *What little fame is left them-just their names*
> *In a few old stories!*

Rather than mistaking the word Fabricius as some critics claim, it is more likely Alfred was demonstrating his knowledge of the legend and of Wayland's Smithy, giving his translation a local flavour to which his audience could relate. But because the legend was from pagan times he had to take care not to make too much of it. What is considered more significant by some is that Alfred was referring to the fact that Wayland's death was not recorded, hence where were his bones? But another possibility is that he was pointing to the confusion that Wayland was supposed to have existed in northern Europe, and now here he was on the Berkshire Downs! This was a logical association of the time, for the dragon in *Beowulf*, a tale probably familiar to the Anglo-Saxons undoubtedly based on earlier tales, although believed to be written not before the eighth century, inhabits a stone burial chamber in a mound; and there are other ancient Scandinavian tales of dragons and giants inhabiting burial bounds to protect the treasure within.

French tales

A sixth century French poem which ranks among the earliest sources refers to a cuirass made by Wieland, the German rendering of Wayland, which protected him from a lance; and the protective powers of Wayland's work were woven into legends of battles against Attila the Hun. In a twelfth-century chronicle of the Counts of Angoulême, Count William received the name of Taillefer, from the French *tailleur* – a hewer, for in a battle against the Normans in single combat with their king he cut the latter's body in two with a single stroke of his sword made by Walander. When Geoffrey Plantagenet, Duke of Normandy, was knighted in 1126, a chronicler records: 'They brought him a sword, taken from the royal treasury, and long since renowned. Galannus, the most skilful of armourers, had employed much care and labour in making it.' There is no doubt that Galannus was the same as Walander.

In fiction there are traces of Wayland everywhere in the romances of chivalry compiled in France in the twelfth and thirteenth centuries, where he is referred to as Galans, Galant, or Galand, where the accent was on swords against which no armour was proof.

In the romance *The Knight of the Swan* Lothaire armed his five sons with five swords from the forge of Galant which he obtained in various battles. Two of them from King Octavian were given to him by Florence, into whose kingdom they had been brought by the Trojans in olden times. One came from a Saracen in Africa, another from the Emir of the Caucasus, and the last was found in the river Jordan. Other brief references are made to swords being of Galant including an alleged brother Dionises, who forged a sword in a cavern in Brittany. This sword Julius Caesar was alleged to eventually possess using it to conquer Europe, and finally it was owned by Espaullars, a hero in the romance. One was said to be possessed by Alexander the Great in his conquests which had passed through the hands of Ptolemy, Judas Maccabeus and the Emperor Vespasian. Although the French romance writers of the Middle Ages used every opportunity to refer to Wayland, they nowhere make any allusion to his adventures as they are recounted in Scandinavian epics.

As Galand he was reintroduced to Britain with the old French romances, but the Anglo-Saxon name of Weland still persisted. In Geoffrey of Monmouth's *Life of Merlin* of the earlier half of the 13th century, a king of Cumberland is made to produce cups sculptured by the hand of Weland, a clear reference to the myth. Here Wayland reverts to the character of goldsmith which is lost in the French romances. But in a fourteenth-century English version of the *Romance of Horn*, maiden Rimnild presents to Horn a sword, 'companion of Miming' and the work of Weland:

> *It is the make of Miming,*
> *Of all swords it is king,*
> *And Weland it wrought.*

Mimung or Mimming was a celebrated sword possibly forged by Mimir, a smith referred to in mediaeval German poetry and who in one saga is Wayland's first teacher, although Wayland is also referred to as its maker. He is presumably to be identified with Mimingus, the 'Satyr of the Woods' in Danish historical romance.

In the fifteenth-century English tale, Gawain, one of King Arthur's Knights of the Round Table, had a sword forged by Galaan inscribed:

> *I am very sharp and hard;*
> *Galaan made me with very great care,*
> *Jesus Christ was fourteen years old when Galaan tempered*
> *and made me.*

Clearly the desire was for a sword which did not bend or snap, and so romances aimed for this all-powerful weapon which only magic could provide. According to Rhenish tales Wayland made his superior swords by filing iron, and mixing the filings with flour and milk fed the mixture to fowls. He then forged the iron anew from the fowl droppings. The same method was recounted on the Euphrates, where tradition likewise had it that the best manufacturers of Baghdad mixed iron fragments with meal and fed it to geese, then using the droppings in the same manner.

The Scandinavian sources

It was once believed the Scandinavian story, as related in the next chapter, was first found at some length in the Icelandic saga, the *Edda*, formerly believed to have been written in the eleventh century, but now considered to be from the beginning of the thirteenth. The *Poetic Edda*, as it is called, which really means Poetic Poetics, was a collection in poetic form of old Norse legends written down by the Icelandic author and historian Snorri Sturlson, who died about 1241. In the *Edda* we are informed Völundarkvida or Wayland was the son of the giant Wade, and that he obtained from the dwergr or dwarves in the interior of the mountains extraordinary skill in the working of metals by fire. Some see the saga as reflecting historical events, mixing history and myth. King Nidung of Nerika in Sweden, who appears as the wicked king Nidud in the saga, appears to have lived in the sixth century and is mentioned as a protector of the Smith. One Danish historian believed Nidung made war upon Weland, prince of Gothland and Scania, for dishonouring his daughter, and surprising him in his territory, made him prisoner.

The German tales

Despite its early references among the Anglo-Saxons the Germans set the scene later than the Scandinavians as the earliest German allusion is in *Walthere* or *Waldhere*, apparently written in the tenth century on the banks of the Rhine. The armour of Walthere, being the work of Weland, is proof against the weapons of the Franks. In the fragment which remains it begins in English:

> ...she encouraged him eagerly: 'Surely the work of Weland will fail not any of men, of those who can hold stout Mimming.' And '...a better sword except the one which I also

have laid at rest in its scabbard set with stones. I know that Theodoric thought of sending it to Widia himself, and also much treasure with the sword, and of decking much beside it with gold. The kinsman of Nitthad, Widia, son of Weland, received the meed for past deeds, because he had delivered him from durance.'

Later references to Weland and his famous sword Mimung or Miming became more frequent in German romances, although there is only one brief reference in one version of the *Nibelungenlied*, the Austrian twelfth- to thirteenth-century epic poem compiled from Frankish, Norse, Bavarian and German lays, based on the destruction of the Burgundian kingdom by the Huns between 437 and 451. In this poem the sword of most renown is Balmung, the sword of Siegfried, lord of the Netherlands, Norway and Nibelungland, stolen by Hagen, his murderer, kinsman and vassal of the Burgundian kings, and surrounding which the bloody events of the poem are set. Siegfried was born in the forest, son of Sigmund, King of Tarlungsland, and Sisibe, daughter of the King of Spain. She places Siegfried in a glass pot and he is accidentally sent floating downstream into the sea. When he reaches the coast he is suckled by a doe and grows very fast. A smith, Mimi, finds him in the forest, names him Siegfried and rears him. As he grows so strong Mimi asks his brother, Regin, a dragon, to kill him But Siegfried beats the dragon to death. Cooking pieces of the dragon to eat he licks broth from his finger and at once understands the conversation of two ravens which are saying he ought to kill Mimi. He then smears his body with the dragon's blood except where he cannot reach between his shoulder blades, and his skin elsewhere becomes horny and impenetrable. Returning home he receives from Mimi a splendid suit of armour and a sword 'Gram', with which he kills Mimi. He then goes to the castle of Brunhild, Queen of Iceland, and obtains the steed Grani which only he can tame. This done he rides away on it and later becomes Theodoric's vassal.

In the saga of Diderich, Dietrich, or Didric of Berne, or Theoderic of Verona, the Ostrogoth, the Germans perhaps set the tale in another country, introducing Wayland's son by Bodvild among the heroes at the court of Dietrich. In this romance we find the adventures of Wieland as in the Scandinavian sagas. Wieland is the son of the giant Wade who himself was born by a sea-sprite Wachitt. Wieland learns the art of a smith from Mimer and afterwards the dwarfs. He goes to King Nidung where he finds another skilful smith, Amilias, whom he kills with his sword Mimung. For punishment the king has him hamstrung. Wieland revenges himself by ravishing the king's daughter and killing his two sons. He then escapes, flying away with wings he had made from feathers. Wittich is the son born to the princess, who obtained a sword from his father and then goes to the court of Dietrich where he distinguishes himself by his exploits with the sword.

In another German poem, Wieland is a duke who has been driven from his country by giants and is obliged to become a smith, first at the court of King Elberich. Afterwards he retreats to the Caucasus mountains. Finally he ends up with King Hertwich or Hertnitt and has a secret liaison with the king's daughter by whom he has two sons, both named Wittich. King Elberich is the dwarf Alfrick, who according to the Wilkina-Saga fabricated the dazzling sword of Ekkisax which became the sword of Theodoric.

In part closer to our own legend of Wayland Smith is that of the Smith of the Hill, a moral tale still prevalent in Lower Saxony at the beginning of the nineteenth century. On the side of a mountain near Osnabruch, which has an extensive cavern, dwelt a smith, a faithful husband, careful father, kind to strangers and one who never turned away a poor wanderer. One Sunday as his wife was returning from church she was struck dead by lightning and the smith cried out against god and enraged with grief would not even see his children again. About a year later he fell into a deadly sickness and at the last hour a strange man of venerable appearance with a long white beard came and carried him into a cavernous cleft in the mountain. Here, for the purification of his soul, working only by night, he was forced to wander and work metals until the mine within was exhausted.

In the mine his good disposition returned to him and he carefully worked the iron ore in preference to gold and silver, making household and agricultural implements, eventually confining his labours to shoeing horses only. Before the cavern was a stake to which the country people tied horses they wished to have shod, but they had to lay the customary fee on a large stone nearby. The Hiller, as they called him, would never be seen by anyone nor disturbed in his cavern.

Time passes and a venturesome fellow decided to enter the cavern, taking with him an armful of green twigs and a lantern. Inside he found passages both left and right so he lay the twigs on the ground as a trail, but his stock was soon exhausted. Nevertheless he decided to continue and came to a lofty iron door, which with two strokes of his axe he forced. As the door flew open the blast of air blew out his lantern. 'Do come in!' shrieked a shrill voice, and stepping forward fearfully he saw strange convulsive images like shadows hovering on the pillars and sides of the cavern. The smith was in the midst of the deformed spirits of the mine. His servants, ranged on both sides, sat on long beams of massive silver amidst shining heaps of gold.

'Now come in friend!' once again screamed the voice, 'take your place at my side.' The man hesitated and the voice shouted: 'Wherefore then so afraid? Take courage, no harm shall happen to thee; as thou camest so shall we send thee back.' The voice then went on to say that discontent about the decline of the man's fortunes had misled him and made him seek after forbidden treasure, 'Dig thy field and garden thoroughly, manure thy meadow and pasture land, so will't thou create for thyself a true gold and silver mine.' The man was then suddenly blasted back outside of the cave, and finding himself at liberty swore he would act according to the advice of the Hiller and never again enter his retreat.

Some say the Hiller eventually lost his obliging disposition and often hurled red-hot ploughshares from on high and kept the peasants in terror without cause, wherefore they conjectured there would soon be an end to him and the mine. The final part of this moral tale perhaps had its origin in the eruption of a volcano.

Other countries' tales

The poem of Frederic of Suabia celebrates Wieland as an amorous adventurer using an alternative version of the *Edda*. The poem on Biterolf first acclaims the sword which this hero bore and which was named Schritt. A weapon without equal, it was fashioned by Mimer the old who dwelt in Azzaria near Toledo. He had no rival but Hertrich in Gascony and later Wieland, who made the sword for his son, the hero Witega. The first two smiths made twelve swords, Wieland made a thirteenth named Mimunc. To bear one of these swords one had to be a prince or the son of a prince.

The *Vaulundurs Saga* by Arnold Oehlenschlager, the Danish romantic writer, is a greatly expanded and modified version of the Wayland tale written in the early nineteenth century and hence no more relating to the original story than Scott's romance, although often repeated as the Wayland legend. And in 1924-28 Kathleen Buck produced her own poem, *The Wayland-Dietrich Saga. The Saga of Dietrich of Bern and his companions Preceded by that of Wayland Smith. Their Deeds in the 4 and 5th Centuries A.D., as told from the 10th to the 13th Centuries. Collected, set in order, and retold in Verse in the 20th Century*. In which, after the first nine volumes, she never got beyond *The Saga of Wayland*.

4

Stories of the Norsemen

'Cut from him the might of his sinews.'

The Poetic Edda

The Lay of Volund

The word *Voelundr* signified a smith in Icelandic and it is from the word *Voelund*, a smith, that the name Weland, and eventually Wayland, derives. Interpretations and embellishments of the mythical legend of Wayland are found in poems and sagas in Iceland, the Faroe Isles, Sweden, Denmark and Germany. In Iceland the name of Weland is attached to superior works of skill and a labyrinth is called a Weland-house. The Swedes have a rock cavern called Verlehall on an island in a lake in the district of Kumevald which they identify as Weland's workshop, and his tomb in some huge stones near Sisebeck in Scania. The village of Veller-by in Jutland also claims the site of his tomb, and in Britain we claim the site of his smithy on the Berkshire Downs.

The first most complete saga that has come down to us, *Völundarkvida* or *The Lay of Volund* in the work known as *The Poetic Edda*, appears to combine two poems, the tale of the valkyries or swan maidens, and Volund's imprisonment and revenge. In the poem Nidud was a Swedish king who had two sons and a daughter Bodvild, variously spelt. The other players were three brothers, Slagfid, Egil and Volund, sons of a Lappish king. Hunting on snowshoes they came to Wolfdale and built themselves a house near a lake called Wolflake. The Icelandic version translates Ulfdal as the Valley of the Bears and Ulfsiar as Bears' Lake, because there were no wolves in Iceland. Early one morning the brothers found three women on the shore spinning. They were valkyries who fly through the air as swans, and near them were their swan's garments. Two were daughters of King Hlodver; Hladgud, the swan-white, and Hervor, the strange creature. The third, Olrun, or all-knowing, was the daughter of Kiar of Valland. The brothers took them home as their wives, Egil taking Olrun, Slagfid Swanwhite, and Volund, Alvit (Hervor); and they lived together for nine winters.

The Valkyrs, or battle maidens, were the attendants of Odin, or Spirit, who created man; supernatural female beings who rode through the sky on white horses, the personification of clouds, wielding swords which created lightning, attending battles, and sweeping down to earth to choose among the heroes those worthy enough to receive the kiss of death and be transported to Valhalla where they would drink heavenly mead:

> *Their horses fetlock-deep in blood, they ride,*
> *And pick the bravest warriors out for death.*
> (Matthew Arnold)

Young and beautiful, with dazzling white arms and flowing golden hair, the Valkyrs were supposed to take frequent flights to earth in swan wings which, according to some versions, they would throw off if they came to a secluded stream, to indulge in bathing. In another version they appeared as swans. Any mortal man surprising them thus and securing the wings could prevent them leaving the earth and force them to succumb to him. They were referred to as spinning flax for they also spun the thread of destiny.

After seven years they became restless, and after nine winters flew off to a battle. Upset at the loss of their wives, Slagfid and Egil went to look for them, while Volund remained at home working with gold and gems and made seven hundred rings which he strung on a piece of bast. Hearing stories of Volund's treasure, when Nidud heard Volund was alone he went at night with his men to the hut. Entering, he saw the seven hundred rings threaded on the bast and taking one put back the remainder, then hid with his men to await Volund's return. Volund came back and began to roast a she-bear he had hunted. Counting his rings he found one missing, but thought his wife must have returned and taken it as a sign. Falling asleep dreaming of her, when he awoke he found he was bound and fettered. Then Nidud, addressing Volund as 'lord of elves', asked him where he had obtained the gold. Volund replied it was not Nidud's nor part of a legendary hoard, but rightfully his own. Nidud answered he must be either a thief or a sorcerer, and taking him prisoner gave to his daughter Bodvild the gold ring, and himself wore Volund's sword. The queen, seeing Volund, says:

> *He is not very gentle, this one who came out of the forest.*
> *He bares his teeth in craving when the sword is shown before him*
> *and he recognizes Bodvild's ring;*
> *similar are his eyes to a shining serpent.*

And she orders he be hamstrung to prevent his escape, and placed on Sævarstadir island. There he laboured incessantly making treasures for the king, who was the only person allowed to visit him, jealous others might steal the treasure. Some versions also have Volund construct a labyrinth, a throwback to one of the original versions in Ancient Greece. A maze in Iceland is known to this day as 'Vælund's House'. Then the king's two sons came secretly to see the treasure stored in a chest, and Volund told them to return another day without telling anyone. When they returned, as they looked inside the chest he cut off their heads and buried their bodies in the mud. The skulls he fashioned with silver, some versions say gold, and gave them to Nidud claiming they were fashioned from rare shells which had washed up on the beach. Their eyes he made like gems, set them in armbands and sent them to the queen. From their teeth he made brooches and sent them to Bodvild.

Then Bodvild broke the ring and went to Volund asking him to repair it, fearful of her father's displeasure if he knew she had damaged it. Volund agreed, but overcame her with beer and ravished her when she fell asleep. Laughing, Volund then rose into the air, possibly having transformed himself into a swan, while Bodvild left in tears fearing her father's wrath. Volund flew to the palace and perching on a wall revealed all to Nidud, adding that Bodvild was with his child but asking that she and the child be not harmed.

This, the basic Scandinavian story, was seemingly later enlarged upon from other sources of the legend.

Volund's revenge

According to one version, after being maimed by Nidud, Volund brooded night and day over his revenge, and then the king brought him the stolen sword for repair. Volund substituted another without magic powers. Further opportunity for revenge presented itself when the king's two sons came secretly to visit him desirous of obtaining some of the wealth in the forge. Demanding the key they opened a chest which was filled with rich and beautiful jewellery. Volund told them the treasure should be theirs if the princes could return the next day in secrecy, which they did early the next morning. Volund was waiting, and shutting the door behind them immediately cut off their heads. Burying the bodies in the marshy ground on which the forge was built, he plated the tops of the skulls with silver and made drinking vessels from them for Nidud's table. Their eyes he dried and fashioned into gems for the queen, and their teeth he filed into pearls and made into a necklace which he sent to the princess Bodvild. But Volund was not yet satisfied with his revenge. Bodvild had broken the ring stolen from Volund which her father had given her, and fearful of his anger went secretly to Volund and demanded he mend it. Volund agreed but asked that she also come secretly to the forge, and when she does he gives her a soporific potion and then ravishes her. After Bodvild had left in tears Volund escaped by flying away using a pair of wings which he had previously fashioned with feathers. But first, grasping the ring and the sword, he flew to the palace. Halting on a wall he called for the king and queen and told them all he had done and that the princess was now pregnant with his child. The King summoned Egil, Volund's brother whom he had in his power, and bade him use his skill as an archer to bring down Volund. Obeying a signal from Volund, Egil aimed at a protuberance under the wing where a bladder full of the young princes' blood was concealed and Volund flew away without hurt, declaring Odin would give his sword to Sigmund, which prophecy ultimately came to pass.

Volund then flew to Alf-heim, where he found his wife again and lived on with her in happiness. But he continued to ply his craft, constructing suits of impenetrable armour and celebrated swords, the most famous being Mimung.

In the German saga of Dietrich of Berne, leader of the Wild Hunt, Wayland dwelt in Heligoland with his son Wittich or Witig. The latter, determined to try his strength against the hero of Bern, persuaded his father to give him the celebrated sword of Mimung. Wayland also fashioned a complete suit of armour for his son and sent him on his way, but the son was defeated by Dietrich and joined him as one of his most trusted knights. Later, pursued by Dietrich he plunges into the sea. According to the Swedish version, his grandmother, the sea-woman, appears to him and conducts him safe and sound to Seeland, where he flourishes for a long time.

The mountain of the dwarfs

In one later compilation, the *Wilkina-Saga*, that is to say the Saga of King Wilkin of Winkinaland in Sweden, believed to have been composed in Norway in the fifteenth century, we learn of a king in Sweden named Wilkin, who while on an expedition formed a liaison with a sea-woman, a spirit of the sea who appears on land as a beautiful woman, who gave birth to Wade, an Alf or supernatural being, sometimes referred to as a giant. His father gave him twelve estates in Seeland, Iceland, where he lived and had a son called Volund or Vaulundr. When Volund was nine years old his father took him to a famous smith of Hunaland called Mimer, to learn metalcraft. After three years there Wade took him to a mountain called Kallova, the interior of which was inhabited by two dwarfs who could forge iron better than the other dwarfs or any other man, and make armaments and jewellery in gold and silver. They undertook to teach Volund all they knew in twelve months, Wade paying them a mark of gold. Volund soon learned all they had to teach him, and when his father came to take him away the dwarfs offered, in their turn, a mark of gold to keep him for another year. Wade agreed, but the dwarfs then repented their extravagance and added that if Wade did not take away his son on the appointed day, they would kill him. Wade agreed but secretly buried a sword at the foot of the mountain, instructing Volund to kill himself if he did not come rather than be killed by the dwarfs, whose jealousy he had excited by becoming so skilful. To this Volund agreed. As the day of his departure approached, Wade, in order to be on time, started his journey three days before the agreed date, but arriving at the mountain found the entrance closed, and being tired he lay down and fell asleep. During his sleep a violent storm arose and he was buried under a fall of earth. The appointed day having arrived the dwarfs came out of the mountain but did not see Wade, and Volund after having sought for him in vain recovered the buried sword. Hiding it under his garments he followed the dwarfs back into the cavern and cut their throats. Then he took their tools and loaded a horse with as much gold as he could carry and took the road to Denmark. Coming to a river named Visara he felled a tree, hollowed it out, placed his treasures and provisions in it, and then got in it himself in a place the water could not penetrate. He then floated towards the sea.

One day the king of Jutland, Nidung, was fishing with his court, when they netted a curiously hewed tree trunk. They were about to cut it open when a voice from within asked them not to, whereupon fearing a sorcerer was hidden inside all but the king ran away.

When Volund emerged he told the king he was not a magician and if the king would spare his life and his treasures, he would render him great services. The story then has many embellishments concerning Volund working for the king, and eventually, because Volund replaced a magic knife with another similar in appearance at the king's table, the king caused him to be hamstrung and the nerves of his feet cut, laming him for life. Volund told the king that if he would restore him to favour he would manufacture for him whatever he required. The king agreed and had a forge built for him where Volund worked all sorts of precious things.

Some time later the king's daughter broke a precious ring and sent to Volund asking him to repair it without her father's knowledge. Volund insisted she come herself as he could not do anything without the king's permission. When she entered the forge Volund fastened the door and ravished her. Shortly after this the king's two sons asked him to make them some arrows. Again he said they would have to come in person, which they did, and once inside the forge he killed them and buried the bodies. He then made drinking cups of their skulls, fashioned their bones into salt cellars and other vases, mounting them in gold and silver, and gave them to the king. He then asked his brother Egil, famed as the most skilful archer of his time, who was held in the king's court, to provide him with feathers of all sizes. Egil went into the woods and killed many birds, bringing the feathers to Volund. Volund fashioned them into wings and encouraged his brother to try them out on the mountain, but Egil fell, narrowly escaping breaking his neck. Volund said he would correct the defect.

Predicting she would give birth to a son, Volund told the king's daughter to bring him up with care and when he was old enough to bear arms to tell him to go in quest of the arms his father had prepared for him. Volund then went to the roof of the house and ascended into the air, telling his brother if ordered to shoot at him to aim at a bladder under his left arm which was filled with the blood of the king's sons. Flying to the highest tower he called out to the king, and told him that because he had been hamstrung he revenged himself upon the king's daughter; and because of cutting the nerves in his feet he had killed his two sons, cutting their throats. The king ordered Egil to shoot him and Egil shot at the bladder of blood, the blood spilling to the earth.

'It is good,' said the king, 'Volund cannot go far.' But he flew to Seeland, descended into a wood and constructed himself a dwelling.

Dwarfs and elves

Walt Disney obtained his inspiration for *Snow White and the Seven Dwarfs* from the fairy tale of the brothers Grimm. Although based on Teutonic folklore none of the tales reflects the Wayland Smith legend, but the name Snow White perhaps came from Swanwhite, and the seven little dwarfs dug in the mountains for minerals. The story of Snow White is also, like the Wayland legend, a story of envy, jealousy and cruelty. Although the dwarfs in the Snow White story were friendly creatures, in mythology they were not, and they were far removed from the lovable characters Disney painted.

While the gods were occupied in creating the earth and providing for its illumination, a whole host of maggot-like creatures had been breeding in the flesh of Ymir, giant of fire and ice. These uncouth beings now attracted divine attention and the gods gave them superhuman intelligence and divided them into two classes. Those which were dark, treacherous and cunning by nature were banished to Svart-alfa-heim, the undergound home of the black dwarfs, from whence they were never allowed to come forth during the day under penalty of being turned into stone. These dwarfs spent all of their time exploring the hidden recesses of the earth collecting gold, silver and precious stones which they stored away in secret crevices for future use. They wore red caps, their eyes were red and they had black tongues which flickered in and out like that of a snake.

The others became elves, and went to live in Alf-heim or home of the light-elves, situated between heaven and earth – a place whence the elves could flit downwards whenever they pleased to attend the plants and flowers, sport with birds and butterflies, or dance in the silvery moonlight on the green.

Interestingly enough, Stone Age flint arrow-heads were once known in England as 'elf-darts'.

5

Scott's Story

'…my fame haunts the Vale of the Whitehorse…'

Kenilworth

Sir Walter Scott's tale of course bears little resemblance to the original legend. Lancelot Wayland is an ordinary man who makes use of the legend, while his imp, Flibbertigibbet, is simply a local urchin who knows of Lancelot Wayland's secret existence on the Berkshire Downs. In the story, Scott's Elizabethan hero, Tressilian, leaving Cumnor for Marlborough, misses the road at night and ends up in the Vale of Whitehorse. His horse having slipped a shoe he searches for a smith, and told of Wayland by a cottager is introduced to her lodger, a schoolmaster, whom he asks to take him to Wayland. Wayland, the schoolmaster explains, having once been the apprentice of a white wizard, Doctor Doboobie, who disappeared, set himself up in his former master's shop, but not attracting any customers took to shoeing horses, at which he was adept. But he took no money nor did he show himself to anyone.

'…his journey proceeded so slowly, that morning found him only in the Vale of Whitehorse, memorable for the defeat of the Danes in former days, with his horse deprived of a forefoot shoe… The residence of a smith was his first object of enquiry, in which he received little satisfaction from the dullness or sullenness of one or two peasants. He dismounted and walked to a little hamlet where Tressilian asked of a dame whether there was a smith in the neighbourhood.

Fig. 18. Cruikshank's impression of Flibbertigibbet.

Speaking it seems with a Scottish accent rather than the broad Berkshire brogue:

The dame looked him in the face with a peculiar expression, as she replied, 'Smith! Ay, truly is there a smith – what wouldst ha' wi' un, mon?'
'To shoe my horse, good dame,' answered Tressilian; 'you may see that he has thrown a forefoot shoe.'

Whereupon the dame, whose name we learn was Gammer Sludge, calls to a Master Holiday within:

'Here's a mon would go to Wayland Smith, and I care not to show him the way to the devil – his horse hath cast a shoe.'

The man, who is a schoolmaster, comes out and addresses Tressilian in Latin. Pleased with being answered in the same language he listens to Tressilian's request and invites him to breakfast. He eventually explains that two or three years before a Doctor Doboobie came to those parts, a white witch who received acclaim for his treatments but then suddenly disappeared. He had a servant, Wayland, employed in trimming his furnace, compounding his drugs, etc. This Wayland assumed the trade of his master but the people were not impressed, so being a skilful farrier he took to shoeing horses but would take no money for it, nor show himself to any man. Refusing to show Tressilian the way, the schoolmaster says that he will send the son of Gammer Sludge, Dickie Sludge, to point the way without approaching the dwelling. The latter agrees on payment of a groat, and Tressilian accompanies his 'elvish guide', whose playmates call him Hobgoblin because of his ugly looks (Fig. 18). Eventually his guide announces they are at Wayland Smith's forge door:

> 'You jest, my little freind,' said Tressilian; 'Here is nothing but a bare moor, and that ring of stones, with a great one in the midst, like a Cornish barrow.'
>
> 'Ay, and that great flat stone in the midst, which lies across the top of these uprights', said the boy, 'is Wayland Smith's counter, that you must tell down your money upon.'
>
> 'What do you mean by such folly?' said the traveller, beginning to be angry with the boy, and vexed with himself for having trusted such a hare-brained guide.
>
> 'Why,' said Dickie, with a grin, 'you must tie your horse to that upright stone that has the ring in't, and then you must whistle three times, and lay me down your silver groat on that other flat stone, walk out of the circle, sit down on the west side of that little thicket of bushes, and take heed you look neither to right nor to left for ten minutes, or so long as you shall hear the hammer clink, and whenever it ceases, say your prayers for the space you could tell a hundred, or count over a hundred, which will do as well, and then come into the circle; you will find your money gone and your horse shod.'

Tressilian doesn't believe him and chases him intending to beat him, but unable to catch the boy Dickie taunts him from the top of a

Top: Fig.19. Artist's impression in Kenilworth, circa 1890. The "smithy".
Bottom: Fig. 20. Artist's impression in Kenilworth, circa 1890. Wayland threatens Flibbertigibbet and Tressilian.

hillock. Eventually they come to an agreement and Tressilian agrees to do as requested. After Dickie whistles, because Tressilian could not whistle loudly enough, they both sit down behind a bush (Fig. 19). Soon they begin to hear the stroke of a hammer as of a farrier at work, but Tressilian thinks this some kind of trick and as soon as the sound finishes, instead of waiting runs round the thicket sword in hand. There he confronts a man in a farrier's leather apron, but otherwise fantastically attired in a bear-skin dressed with the fur on, and a cap of the same, which almost hid the sooty and begrimed features of the wearer (Fig. 20). The boy urges Tressilian to come back as the smith heaves up his hammer ready to do battle, and calls out,

'Wayland, touch him not, or you will come by the worse! The gentleman is a true gentleman, and a bold.'

'So thou has betrayed me, Flibbertigibbet?' said the smith; 'it shall be the worse for thee!'

Tressilian then browbeats Wayland into talking as a man and asks him to explain why he behaves as he does. This they decide to do in Wayland's den. The smith reveals a trapdoor covered with bushes and lifting it, disappears below. The other two then follow, descending a short and narrow staircase into a small square vault, containing a forge and, besides the farrier's accoutrements, an alchemist's crucibles, retorts and other instruments (Fig. 21). Wayland reveals he was a travelling juggler three years before and met Tressilian in Devonshire. Bred a blacksmith he tired of it and became apprentice to a juggler, later becoming one in his own right performing in Tressilian's presence. After that he had turned to the stage but soon tired of it and became attached to a physician, a Doctor Doboobie, who was also an alchemist and astrologer, who built the secret underground laboratory which they were in, where he absented himself from the town of Faringdon. Believed to be a sorcerer he became cursed and threatened whenever he shewed himself in the streets, and so one day departed, leaving everything to Wayland, who had become known as the devil's foot-post, and likewise could not show his face in the village without receiving a volley of stones.

Fig.21. Artist's impression in Kenilworth, circa 1890. Wayland in his cave with Flibbertigibbet and Tressilian.

The furnace, which had been extinguished, he found booby-trapped with a barrel of gunpowder, so he did not attempt any alchemy and wished instead to revert to being a blacksmith, but none would bring a horse to be shod by the devil's assistant.

Meanwhile, when at Faringdon with his master, he had made friends with Dickie Sludge by teaching him a few secrets, and the latter agreed to spread the tale about the invisible smith. Now he feared what might happen if the people discovered it was he all along. Tressilian offers to take him with him and insists he first don normal clothes and clean himself up. They then say farewell to Dickie Sludge and trot off, Wayland having his own horse which he retrieved from nearby. When they had gone nearly a mile they heard a tremendous explosion and turned to see a huge pillar of dark smoke rising into the sky from the spot they had just left. Wayland guessed that Dickie Sludge had blown up the cavern with the keg of gunpowder from mischieviousness. They then travel towards Devonshire, stopping at Marlborough where they find the news had already preceded them. Asking a hostler the man replied, 'But here was a rider but now, who says the devil hath flown away with him they called Wayland Smith, that won'd about three miles from the Whitehorse of Berkshire, this very morning, in a flash of fire and a pillar of smoke, and rooted up the place he dwelt in, near that old cockpit of upright stones...'

It is not long before they are to make a return journey through Berkshire and Tressilian wonders whether Wayland might not be recognized. The latter replies, 'I warrant me, my fame haunts the Vale of the Whitehorse long after my body is rotten; and that many a lout ties up his horse, lays down his silver groat, and pipes like a sailor whistling in a calm, for Wayland Smith to come and shoe his tit for him...'

'In this particular, indeed, Wayland proved a true prophet; and so easily do fables rise, that an obscure tradition of his extraordinary practice in farriery prevails in the Vale of Whitehorse even unto this day; and neither the tradition of Alfred's Victory (s), nor of the celebrated Pusey Horn*, are better preserved in Berkshire than the wild legend of Wayland Smith.'

---

* In the eleventh century King Canute is said to have occupied Cherbury Camp in Berkshire (now Oxfordshire), while the Anglo-Saxons under Ethelred were gathered on White Horse Hill, seven miles away. One of Canute's officers, William Pusey, entered the enemy camp in the disguise of a shepherd and learnt of a proposed ambush, returned and warned Canute. In return the king gave William an ox horn and the land over which the sound of the horn could be heard. The tenure thus established was known as cornage or horngeld, one of the oldest forms of title deed. The alleged original horn, one of five similar cornage horns in existence, was held by the Pusey family until the nineteenth century but is now in the Victoria and Albert Museum.

Postscript

In the Early Bronze Age, four thousand three hundred years ago give or take 150 years, a young man in his early twenties, young to us but in his day already approaching middle-age, left his home in the Swiss Alps and set out on a journey across Europe. We like to think he knew the art of smelting and working precious metals of copper and gold, an art making him revered as a magician among the peoples he met on his journey, still labouring away with implements of stone. To impress them, across his chest he displayed a gleaming dagger fashioned of shiny copper which had come from far away near the Spanish coast, but of a metal too soft to be of any real use as a weapon. In his hand he carried a long bow to protect himself against the bear and the wolf and any hostile people he might come across, and to provide himself with food.

As he wandered far and wide impressing the wild people with his skill, wondrous tales were passed by word of mouth the length and breadth of Europe of this fabulous smith, becoming embellished in the telling, recounting stories of people who dwelt in caves in the remote fastness of the Alps and the wonderful treasures they could make. Coming to a great lake (it was in fact the sea) our wandering smith decided to try his luck in a land where none knew of such skills and from whence came tales of a great monument being built, which we came to know as Stonehenge. And it was three miles from Stonehenge near the village of Amesbury that his grave was found in May 2002. By now aged 35 to 45 years, he died about the time the great stones were being erected. Buried with him were two decorative hammered gold ornaments which he would have worn in tresses in his hair, fashioned with gold from southern Europe; three copper daggers, his bow, flint arrowheads, sundry earthen beakers that once would have contained food for him to take into the next world, and a cushion stone for hammering out on the precious metals. Nearby was the grave of his son of 20 to 25 years who had worn identical gold ornaments. The son was probably brought up in the Midlands or north-east Scotland, so the smith must have wandered far and wide before coming to Stonehenge.

With a festering abscess in his lower jaw the smith would have been an ill-tempered man, but what is more he was lame, the kneecap severed from his left leg and the wound now several years old with an infection in the bone giving added constant pain. The injury is the sort that might have been made in confrontation with a wounded bear, for it would take an odd stroke to make such a cut in a fight, and if it had indeed been so, how come he was not finished off? Unless others saved him. But he bore no weapon for real close combat or we might have expected such to be buried with him.

Misleadingly known as the 'Amesbury archer', for the bow was simply for his protection or for hunting, what is the significance of this remarkable find, apart from being the most complete Bronze Age burial discovered? Apparently a worker in precious metals, from the mountains of central Europe, who makes his way to a lake in the north armed with a bow and later is lamed. Surely all the components of the legend of Wayland Smith? Could not this Bronze Age man, quite coincidentally to the proximity of Wayland's Smithy which would have adopted the legend nearly three thousand years later, have been the prototype of the myth? A myth which derived not from Norsemen, nor even the Myceneans, but from the stories of the magical powers associated with the first Bronze Age workers in precious metals.

The Antiquary's Bookshelf

Akerman, J. Y. 1847. 'Observations on the celebrated Monument at Ashbury, in the county of Berks, called 'Wayland Smith's Cave'.' *Archaeologia*. xxxii: 312-314.

Atkinson, R. J. C. 1965. 'Wayland's Smithy'. *Antiquity*. xxxix: 126-133.

Bayley, M. 1996. Kecks, Keddles and Kesh: Celtic Language, Lovespoons and the Cog Almanac. Milverton: Capall Bann Publishing.

Donaldson, T. L. 1862. 'Wayland Smith's cave or cromlech, near Lambourn, Berks'. *The Wiltshire Archaeological and Natural History Magazine*. VII: 315-320.

Grinsell, L. V. 1936. *The Ancient Burial Mounds of England*. Methuen & Co. Ltd., London.

Hutchinson, H. G. ed. 1904. *Letters and Recollections of Sir Walter Scott by Mrs. Hughes (of Uffington)*. London: Smith, Elder & Co.

Lewis, A. H. 1869. 'On Certain Druidic Monuments in Berkshire'. In: International Congress of Prehistoric Archæology: *Transactions of the Third Session which Opened at Norwich on the 20th August and Closed in London on the 28th August 1868*. Longmans, Green and Co., London.

Palmer, M. 2002. *The Sacred History of Britain*. Piatkus, London.

Singer, S. W. 1847. *Wayland Smith. A Dissertation on a Tradition of the Middle Ages. From the French of G.B.Depping and Francisque Michel. And the Amplified Legend by Oehlenschlager*. London: William Pickering.

Thurnam, J. 1862. 'On Wayland's Smithy, and on the Traditions connected with it'. *The Wiltshire Archaeological and Natural History Magazine*. VII: 321-333.

Whittle, A., Brothwell, D., Cullen, R., Gardner, N. and Kerney, M. P. 1991. 'Wayland's Smithy, Oxfordshire: Excavations at the Neolithic Tomb in 1962-63 by R. J. Atkinson and S. Piggott'. *Proceedings of the Prehistoric Society*. 57(2):61-101.

Wise, F. 1738. *A letter to Dr Mead concerning some Antiquities in Berkshire, Particularly shewing that The White Horse, which gives name to the Vale, is a Monument of the West-Saxons, made in memory of a great Victory obtained over the Danes A.D. 871*. Thomas Wood, Oxford.

Wright, T. 1847. 'On the Legend of Weland the Smith'. *Arch*. 315-324.

Wright, T. 1860. 'On the legendary History of Wayland Smith'. *The Journal of the British Archaeological Association*. XVI:50-58.

Index

Akerman, J. Y. 27
Alfred, King 61-62
Allen, Grant 38-39
Amesbury archer 86-87
Anglo-Saxons 8, 10
Anglo-Saxon Charters 13, 40; Poetry 60
Arnold, Matthew 71
Ashbury 7
Ashdown House 17; Park 22
Ashmole, Elias 17
Aubrey, John 17-18, 24, 49, 50
Avebury 19-22
Axe, Cornish stone 42; flint 42

Barham, Richard 11
Barrow, long 7, 41; construction 43-49; round 4; unchambered 42-43; use of 53
Bayley, Michael 9, 33, 35, 47
Beaghild's burial place 14
Beowulf 14, 41, 47, 60-61
Berkshire Downs 1, 7, 41, 70
Blowing Stone 23
Bodies 44-45
Bodvild 14, 70, 72, 73
Boethius 61-62
Book of Days, The 28-29, 31-32
Britannia 11, 16
Buck, Kathleen 69

Camden, William 11, 16
Chalmers, Mary 38
Clinch, George 7
Compton Beauchamp 13; church 37

Cork, Job 35-36
Craven, Lord 27, 36
Currency bars 55, 57

Daedalus 60
Deor 61
Dietrich Saga 67, 74
Donaldson, Prof. 27, 38, 51-53
Downland Man 38
Dwarfs 74-75

Edda 61, 65, 69, 70
Egil 74, 76
Egypt 50
Excavations 42, 53

Flibbertigibbet 35
Franks casket 15-16
Frederic of Suabia 69
French tales 63-64
Funerary practice 50

Galand 64
Galannus 63
Gawain 64
Gotland 40
Grave goods 45
Greek mythology 58
Grinsell, L. V. 33
Grimm brothers 77

Halton, Lancashire 39-40
Hearne, Thomas 24-25
Hoare, Sir Richard 51
Hughes, family 11; Mrs. 11, 12, 35-36;

Thomas 1, 11

Ingoldsby Legends 11
Iron Age 54

Kenilworth 10, 11, 12, 36, 78-85

Land changes 53-54
Lay of Volund, The 70-73
Leland, John 39
Lewis, A. L. 22-23, 27, 53
Looting 54
Lyson's *Magna Britannia* 26-27

Massingham, H. J. 19, 20, 38-39
Mastaba 50
Miller, Reverend H. 35
Mimung (mimming) 64, 66
Mirror of Literature, The 27
Mummification 45, 46, 50

Neolithic 41
Nidud 63, 70
Niebelungenlied 66

Odin 8, 40, 71
Odstone (Oldstone) Farm, 33
Oehlenschlager, Arnold 69

Palmer, Martin 53
Picture stones 40
Pusey horn 85, 85n
Pyramids 50

Ridgeway 3, 7, 41
Ring ditch 41
Risborough 40
Romano-British period 54

Sacrificial altars 38
Sarsen stones 22
St. Peter, Church of 39

Satanist services 37-38
Scandinavian sources 65
Scott, Sir Walter 10-12, 24, 32, 33, 35-36, 78
Siegfried 66; saga 40
Skeletons 49, 53
Skemming 8
Sleipnir 8, 40
Smith, Dr. Elliot 50
Smith of the Hill 67-69
Smith, R. A. 55
Snivelling Corner 33, 35; Stone 11
Snow White 77
Stonehenge 41
Stukeley, Reverend William 24
Sword manufacture 64-65

Thurnam, Dr. 38
Tomb robbers 14
Trees 27
Trenches 54
Teutonic folklore 1, 60, 77

Uffington Castle 3

Valkyries 70, 71
Vaulundurs Saga 69
Victoria County History of Berkshire 7
Voelundr 60, 70
Völundarkvida 70
Vulcan 58-60

Wade 39, 65, 67, 74-75
Walt Disney 77
Walthere (Waldhere) 65
Wayland, derivation of name 60, 70; Hundred of 40; legends 70-74; Pond 40
Wayland Smith 1, 3, 11; legend 3, 7, 9, 15, 24, 32, 50
Wayland Smith's Cave 3
Wayland's Folly 27

Wayland's Smithy 1, 7, 13, 41, 62; construction 47, 49; first record 13
Weathercock Hill 41
Weland 1
White Horse 1, 8, 10
Wieland 64, 67, 69
Wilkina Saga 74–76
Williams, Alfred 33
Wise, Francis 18, 23-24, 27, 38, 50-51
Witches' Moon-dial 38
Wittich's Hill 14

Ymir 77
Yorkshire 39

ALSO PUBLISHED BY THE WYCHWOOD PRESS

May Day to Mummers
Folklore and traditional customs in Oxfordshire

CHRISTINE BLOXHAM

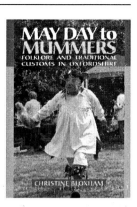

This fascinating, detailed and highly entertaining book is the definitive account of the customs and festivities that took place in Oxfordshire before the days of mass entertainment.

Traditions dovetailed neatly into the farming year. Recreation and celebration, coupled with practices relating to fertility of both crops and people, often harked back to pre-Christian times: their evolution is evidence of changing religious beliefs and social patterns. Traditions could also provide an opportunity for making money, perhaps for a good cause (such as the whit ales that raised money for the parish) or for private gain (as when morris dancers toured the countryside or children made May garlands to show).

Among **hundreds of different customs** described, often in the words of contemporary sources from the last 400 years, particular mention should be made of the very many customs associated with **May Day**, the strong **morris** tradition that survives in certain towns and villages, the **mock mayor-making** in Abingdon, Banbury, Oxford and Woodstock, the **Burford dragon ceremony**, various traditions of **beating the bounds**, the **mummers plays** that are still performed, **bun throwing in Abingdon**, and the ritual of **'hunting the mallard'** that takes place once a century at All Souls College, Oxford.

The book includes **the text of two mummers' plays** (from Islip, dating from about 1780, and Westcott Barton, recorded in 1870) and a **Christmas miracle play** collected in Thame in 1853.

Includes many rare and unusual photographs, as well as photographs of modern revivals of ancient customs.

Christine Bloxham is a former assistant keeper of antiquities at the Oxfordshire Museum. Her previous books include *The World of Flora Thompson* (1998). She has been collecting local folklore for thirty years.

£12.99 pbk 320pp 1-902279-11-5

Iron Age and Roman Wychwood
The land of Satavacus and Bellicia

Tim Copeland

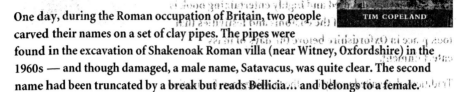

One day, during the Roman occupation of Britain, two people carved their names on a set of clay pipes. The pipes were found in the excavation of Shakenoak Roman villa (near Witney, Oxfordshire) in the 1960s — and though damaged, a male name, Satavacus, was quite clear. The second name had been truncated by a break but reads Bellicia... and belongs to a female.

Besides possibly identifying a lover and his lass, both names are from the pre-Roman Iron Age tradition, even though the pipes were found in the debris of a building that was dated to almost two hundred years after the Roman invasion. The names on the pipes demonstrate continuity between the people living in Wychwood before the arrival of the Romans and those who worked the land for centuries after that event.

Today's roads and parish boundaries, the location of villages and the distribution of vegetation have evolved in part from decisions taken to meet the needs of inhabitants in the period 800 BC – 400 AD.

This profusely illustrated book is about the evidence in Wychwood for the Iron Age and Roman periods, including hill forts, Akeman Street, Grim's Ditch, Roman villas, religious sites, and much besides. It also chronicles the evolution of our understanding of the period by examining the records and conclusions of archaeologists over the centuries, showing how their findings were shaped by their historical and cultural assumptions and the scientific tools at their disposal.

Includes a gazeteer of Iron Age and Roman remains that can be seen and accessed from public land, and a great deal of information for people visiting West Oxfordshire and the sites described.

Tim Copeland is Head of the International Centre for Heritage Education at the University of Gloucester, Chairman of the Council of Europe's Cultural Heritage Expert Committee and a Fellow of the Society of Antiquaries. Recent and forthcoming publications include work for the Council of Europe, the National Trust, the Royal Fine Art Commission and English Heritage.

£12 pbk 144pp, with b/w photographs, maps and line drawings 1-902279-14-X

For a complete catalogue of books published by The Wychwood Press,
phone 01608 811969